What people are saying about . . .

D1434732

10,000 REASONS

"I am so grateful that God puts songs in our heart and lyrics on our lips to express what is in the deepest part of us. '10,000 Reasons' is undoubtedly a song that was sent from heaven. I most love how it reminds me every day I have countless reasons to praise our great God. The stories Matt captures here from the impact of this song are so beautiful and powerful. However, this book could never have enough pages to tell of just what God has done through this simple yet profound chorus and three verses. I believe wholeheartedly this song will echo into generation after generation. God gave Matt this song and the ministry that has come with it because He knew Matt could be trusted. I can't imagine a greater endorsement than that!"

Chris Tomlin, worship leader and songwriter

"My friend Matt Redman has the coolest 'God moment' stories. I've tried many times to retell his stories to others, with the caveat 'I really wish you could hear Matt tell it—it's much better.' Well, now you can hear him tell it. And he shapes his words for the page just as beautifully as he crafts anthems for the church."

Steven Furtick, pastor of Elevation Church
and *New York Times* bestselling author

"Life is a mixture of desire and death, laughter and loss. At some point, we all find ourselves in dark passageways, confused about how we arrived there and unsure of the way out. The song '10,000 Reasons' is a juggernaut of faith that strangles gloom and gives breath to the weary—as well as to the winning. This powerful book celebrates the stories the song has spawned around the globe. If you've found refuge in the song, these stories are going to cause you to erupt once more with applause for our great God."

Louie Giglio, speaker at Passion Conferences
and pastor of Passion City Church

"Matt Redman is one of the most brilliant Spirit-filled songwriters of our generation. People will still be singing '10,000 Reasons' one hundred years from now should Jesus tarry. Matt's book *10,000 Reasons* will edify you as his hymn does. The testimonies will bring you to tears. You won't be able to put it down."

R. T. Kendall, minister emeritus of
Westminster Chapel, London

"We are huge fans of this book about a song we love to lead, by a man we love to follow. It is impossible not to recommend this quotable, entertaining, and often moving resource."

Rend Collective, worship community band

"There are so many things we love about Matt Redman—his heart, his songs, the way he leads us in worship. But one of my favorite things is the way he is willing to open up his life story for us to learn and glean from, always pointing us to Jesus and always declaring the faithfulness of God. He writes with an authority known only to one who has truly walked through the fire and yet all the while experiences firsthand God's abiding presence. This book will inspire and champion your heart to draw closer to Christ, whatever season you are walking through."

Darlene Zschech, worship leader and author

10,000 REASONS

10,000 REASONS

STORIES OF FAITH, HOPE, AND THANKFULNESS
INSPIRED BY THE WORSHIP ANTHEM

MATT REDMAN
WITH CRAIG BORLASE

David C Cook

transforming lives together

10,000 REASONS
Published by David C Cook
4050 Lee Vance View
Colorado Springs, CO 80918 U.S.A.

David C Cook U.K., Kingsway Communications
Eastbourne, East Sussex BN23 6NT, England

The graphic circle C logo is a registered trademark of David C Cook.

The website addresses recommended throughout this book are offered as a
resource to you. These websites are not intended in any way to be or imply an
endorsement on the part of David C Cook, nor do we vouch for their content.

Details in some stories have been changed to protect
the identities of the persons involved.

Bible credits are listed in the back matter.

"10,000 Reasons" by Matt Redman © 2011 sixstepsrecords/Sparrow Records.

LCCN 2016938479
ISBN 978-1-4347-0290-6
eISBN 978-1-4347-1088-8

© 2016 Matt Redman and Craig Borlase

Cover Artwork: Cindy Hong

The Team: Kyle Duncan, Amy Konyndyk, Nick Lee, Jack Campbell, Susan Murdock
Cover Design: Leighton Ching

Printed in the United States of America
First Edition 2016

1 2 3 4 5 6 7 8 9 10

052616

This book is dedicated to my stunning and inspiring wife, Beth—and to my children, Maisey, Noah, Rocco, Jackson, and Levi. I love the adventure that songs like this have led us on together. Thanks for making the hard moments more bearable and the fun moments even more enjoyable. I love you so much. Also, thanks to Jonas for being a brilliant friend and a fantastic songwriting partner. You're a part of all the stories of faith that are in this book.

CONTENTS

FOREWORD

The Blanco River typically meanders through south Texas like a sleepy summer afternoon. But every so often, it gets angry. Just ask Jonathan McComb. He, his family, and his friends had nothing more in mind than a peaceful Memorial Day weekend of play and rest. But the river had other plans.

Swollen by spring rains, the river roared forty-four feet over its banks and swept everything in sight into the dark night. Jonathan had little warning and no time to prepare. The river house in which he was staying was sucked off its foundation and carried downriver with residents inside. It crashed into bridges and trees, ripping walls away. Within a few minutes, all inside were desperately clutching to a single mattress. One by one, Jonathan saw his friends, wife, and children lose the battle.

By the time Jonathan was able to clutch a tree and pull himself to shore, he'd suffered unspeakable tragedy. Within a few days he stood before a crowded church and paid eulogy to his wife and two children. Among the songs he chose was Matt Redman's "10,000 Reasons."

Jonathan's story is just one of hundreds already experienced and thousands more yet to be. The hymn will minister to people for generations until our Savior returns. The reason is simple—gratitude in the midst of suffering is its surest remedy. Nothing, I mean nothing, lifts the heavy heart like a heartfelt "Bless the Lord." It is for this reason that Matt's song will endure.

Might I suggest one other reason? Matt himself. He is the kindest, gentlest soul that England has ever produced. One conversation with him is never enough. He has a way of making you feel like you are the only human being on the planet. He's never in a hurry. Never impatient. He genuinely cares about the people who hear his songs.

He cared about Jonathan. Matt and I had participated in an event at Madison Square Garden in New York City. The concert was over and the standing-room-only crowd was still buzzing as I escorted Jonathan through the corridors of the arena. He had flown from Texas with the hope of hearing Matt and thanking him for the song. I stood a few feet at a distance and watched as the lanky cowboy from Texas shared his story with the kind Brit. Matt's eyes widened, then moistened, as he heard Jonathan describe the flood, the loss, and the funeral.

The song had touched yet another life.

The book you hold contains a collage of such stories. As you read them, be thankful for the song, for its writer, and most of all, be thankful for the Savior who inspired it.

He certainly did.

Max Lucado

ACKNOWLEDGMENTS

Craig—you are a true craftsman. I love how you wrestle with words to tell every story in the best possible way. I also love that old school friends get to do something like this together after so many years.

Kyle and the team at David C Cook—thanks for getting this idea off the ground and for your great partnership in this.

A big thanks to my generous friend Max Lucado for the foreword. Your pastoral heart always shines through.

Also, a huge thanks to the many inspiring worshippers who contributed stories to this book. I love how the song "10,000 Reasons" became a way for you to showcase your beautiful hearts of worship for Christ.

Bless the Lord O my soul
O my soul
Worship His holy name
Sing like never before
O my soul
I worship Your holy name

Prologue

THE MOMENT

Songwriters love the *moment*. It's the point in a song's life when everything seems to come together. It's that instant when all those intangible emotions you were feeling have been perfectly distilled and the song begins to seamlessly fill the silence. It's the sense that the dry bones are beginning to stand together and that all of a sudden the song has developed a life of its own.

Sometimes arriving at the *moment* takes time, toil, and struggle—a contending for the life of the song as you wrestle with the true essence of what it is you're seeking to convey. At other times it arrives more easily—a beautifully unannounced entrance that takes your heart by complete surprise. Regardless of whether it's that long-fought tussle or a more effortless discovery, songwriters are always waiting, hoping that the *moment* is about to arrive.

The song "10,000 Reasons" came along late one night. It was at the end of a long day of songwriting with my friend Jonas in the south of England, and the song came without any hint of a struggle at all. There was something beautiful about the simplicity of its birth—an uncomplicated case of "four chords and the truth."

As *moments* go, it was a pretty good one.

But more was on the way. As enjoyable as it can be to shape a little song like this in the midnight hour, you never really can tell what will become of it, or where the song will eventually end up. As it turns out, "10,000 Reasons" has gone further and traveled wider than any other song I've been a part of writing.

I've had the joy of leading "10,000 Reasons" in so many different places: world-renowned venues such as Abbey Road Studios, Madison Square Garden, and Red Rocks; and historic buildings such as Canterbury Cathedral and the Royal Albert Hall.

One of the biggest highlights of all was singing it in a packed-out Times Square alongside well-known evangelist Luis Palau. I was just ten years old when I committed my life to Christ at a rally hosted by Luis in a London football (soccer) stadium. I never dreamed that thirty years later I'd be standing next to him onstage in the heart of New York, leading this song and then having the privilege of introducing him to the crowd. It was one of my favorite times of leading worship, singing alongside the man who had led me to Christ, surrounded by all those iconic lights and billboards.

And then there is the other extreme too, the more private times when I've been able to worship to this song far away from lights and crowds. Just recently two of my closest friends and I stood in a quiet hospital room of a woman whose body was riddled with disease but whose faith was very much on fire. We started up the song, and although I was the one playing the guitar, it soon became clear that she was the real worship leader, as she rose above the obvious challenges of her circumstances and led us to the throne room of God with her heart of trust and praise.

Then there are all the other versions I've had absolutely no hand in. I've heard beautiful renditions of the song that have come from around the world as far away as China, Haiti, and the cramped backstreets of a Mumbai slum. While there's so much that separates my Royal Albert Hall version—with that sixty-piece orchestra and four-hundred-voice choir—from the one belted out by barefoot children in a dusty South African township, those differences are essentially just musical ones. The voicing may be different, but the heartbeat remains the same. It's the sound of the children of God joining together in a simple and raw act of thanks and devotion. And it's still just four chords and the truth.

I've heard so many stories of how this song has shown up in people's lives. It inspires me to see how deep into people's hearts and situations these worship songs can go. Music has an amazing ability to transport hope, joy, and peace just when we need it most.

Since the release of "10,000 Reasons," I've met some truly inspiring worshippers and encountered such powerful offerings of faith. That's why I decided to write this book. I'd love to share some of those stories, as well as speak into the theme of the song and explore the truths that lie behind it. Not because I think we wrote a great song. It's hard to take a bow for something you didn't plan for.

Instead, I hope that these thoughts and stories will encourage you in your own life of worship. I hope they'll inspire you to keep on thanking and trusting God from a deep place, especially in those tough moments of life when the temptation could so easily be to wander from the path of praise.

My conviction is that the greater the storms we face, the louder our songs must be. I hope this book will encourage you to raise your voice ever louder in the worship of Jesus Christ.

As you read through these stories that take place in hospital wards and at gravesides, you'll see that they all have one thing in common: These worshippers are doing far more than singing a song. They are staking their lives on the truth of who they believe God to be, and they are backing up their words in the clearest and most powerful of ways.

All of these stories remind us that worship is always so much more than a song. Singing our praise can be a powerful thing to do, but the call is always to complete the integrity of our offerings with a life of worship.

Psalm 95 shows us a healthy pattern of what that might look like. It begins by calling us to "sing for joy to the LORD"—we break through the silence with a celebration of His goodness. Next, it invites us to "bow down" in reverence, because recognition of the greatness of God must always be in the mix. But it doesn't stop there. In the last stage of worship, the psalm encourages us, "Do not harden your hearts" (NIV). The words move us beyond an outward expression to the very depths of who we are; for true worship will always affect our lives, not just our lips. The psalmist knew full well that worship without change is just a game.

As loudly as we can sing our songs of praise, the real challenge will always be to complete the integrity of our offerings with a walk of worship.

When our deeds outrun our words.

When our lives outweigh our songs.

CHAPTER 1

10,000 REASONS FOR MY HEART TO FIND ...

I have never liked suits.

Given the choice, I'll go for comfort over class any day. Like when I was twenty-one and turned up for a meeting with a church leader who also happened to be the head of a city investment bank. Not quite realizing beforehand how senior his job was, I squeaked my way across the marble lobby wearing jeans and carrying a plastic shopping bag while the security guards stared.

I've always been this way, and it's not about rebellion or disrespect. It's just that I don't like suits.

So I didn't feel 100 percent comfortable as I sat in the back of a fancy car on the way to an award ceremony. The fabric felt like a vice and I couldn't stop yanking at my collar. Beth, my gorgeous wife, and Jonas, one of my very best friends, just looked kindly at me and smiled knowingly. Beth makes everything she wears look like it was tailored just for her, and since Jonas is a highly fashion-savvy creative type, he was completely at ease in his newest outfit too.

"Do you know what you'll say if you win?" said Beth.

I gave her a wink, a smile, and a shrug. It wasn't the first time we'd attended the Grammy Awards. I'd been nominated once before and left that day with nothing more than happy memories of having a great time and seeing some inspiring performances. There was no way I was going to win this time. No way at all. But then again, a part of you always wonders.

Someone once told me that in a situation like this, even if you're convinced that you're not going to win, you should always have some words prepared to save you the embarrassment of having nothing to say. That seemed like a sensible approach. I'd read a quote from the composer Bach on Twitter that morning, reminding us that "music is for the glory of God and the refreshing of the soul." In the unlikely event of an award coming my way, the Bach sound bite seemed like a good nugget of wisdom to memorize.

> No way I was going to win this time. No way at all.

My soul didn't feel all that refreshed as we walked the line into the venue. Between the cameras and the people clutching clipboards and the calls to "turn this way … now this way," it just made me hurry in as quickly as I could. All I wanted to do was sit down and get ready for the pre-telecast-awards part of the evening.

I found some seats way at the rear of the auditorium and went back to doing battle with my collar while we waited for the Grammys to begin. All around us were immaculately dressed people with immaculate smiles getting ready to enjoy the night of their lives. I recognized a few of them and knew that the rest were all bound to be extremely talented musicians, songwriters, and industry executives. Something about being surrounded by this caliber of person told me that my chances of winning were nonexistent.

The lights dimmed, the show began, and finally I felt myself beginning to relax.

AND THE GRAMMY GOES TO ...

I had to jog pretty hard to reach the stage in time when they called my name. All the other winners I'd seen so far had been seated nearer the front. They'd been able to walk up while their music played, handing out high fives and hugs. Not me. I was concentrating on getting there before the "walking" music stopped but with enough breath in my body to be able to speak. And what was that Bach quote again?

In everything that followed—the photos, the interviews, and even another visit to the stage when they called my name for a second time—I started to enjoy myself a little more. After all, it was a night out in Los Angeles with great friends and great music. And I'd had one of the most affirming moments of my life in music.

But every ten minutes or so I would remind myself that none of it—not the awards or the photos or the glamour of the event—was really what mattered most. I was desperate that even though I was leaving with two Grammy Awards I wouldn't become distracted from the things I knew God had called me to do.

Back and forth I went with these thoughts, kind of enjoying the moment but frequently checking my motives. I was trying to work out what it meant to be a worship leader at the Grammy Awards. Was it really okay to receive this kind of accolade when any minister of music knows that getting awards is really not what leading worship is all about? Deep down I think I just wanted to make sure I gave God every ounce of the glory under the glare of those bright LA lights.

Eventually Beth put me straight. "Let's enjoy this moment, Matt. You didn't ask for this and you certainly didn't aim for it either. I don't know how we ended up here, but God has trusted you with this moment. So let's enjoy it."

I thought back to the beginnings of the song, the very reason I was dressed up in the first place. I remembered being with Jonas alone in a little English chapel, a place where I'd written many songs over the previous decade. The century-old walls had been dancing all evening in the candlelight, and by 1:30 a.m. all I wanted to do was blow out the flames and go home to bed.

We'd both wanted to use the lyrics "bless the Lord" at the heart of a song.

Jonas wouldn't let me. He insisted that I listen to a very early idea he had for a song. It was just a simple melody that started out by climbing three notes up then three notes down, but it was enough to banish the tiredness from my eyes and make me take notice.

For a couple of years we'd both wanted to use the lyrics "bless the Lord" at the heart of a song, and as Jonas ran through the cascading riff on the piano, I knew we'd found it. "Let's bless the Lord!" I shouted. We sang it out loud together. It was an instant fit.

We carried on. The white walls glowed bright as melodies filled the air. The tune was simple, a steady march that stuck close to a few simple notes before building back up to Jonas's initial idea for the chorus melody.

Along with that melody came the lyrics. Those first couple of verses flowed out of us nearly as fast as we could write them down. I'm not sure I really knew where they were heading at the time, but as I typed those phrases that spoke of new days dawning and evening time coming, it just all poured out of us.

Within no more than an hour and a half the song was well on its way to being finished. We blew out the candles and left that chapel feeling a little tired but profoundly grateful to God for the chance to enjoy this new creation, and the sweetness of the *moment*.

BEYOND AWARDS

Remembering the way "10,000 Reasons" was written in that quaint old chapel helped me find my balance again during the glitzy Grammy night in 2012. *Maybe this isn't the most important part of my life*, I thought. *But it's for sure a part of what God's trusting me with.* So I relaxed a little, stopped worrying so much, and embraced the moment.

A friend who works in the music industry came up and said hi. He asked if I'd voted and I told him I had. "Good job too," he said.

"Why?"

"Because that second award you walked away with was a tie. You wouldn't have won if you hadn't have voted."

"Um. I didn't vote for myself."

He looked confused. "What do you mean?"

"It said on the form that you shouldn't let your vote be swayed by someone if you know them. I'm pretty sure that I know myself, so I just didn't vote in the categories that I was nominated in. I thought that was the right thing to do."

"No, you ridiculous Brit," he said, clapping his hands on his face. "Everyone votes for themselves!"

I'm not sure if that's true or not, but I smiled and wondered if heaven was smiling over that little moment too. The fact is, the guys I'd tied with were dear friends of mine, and I love that we got to share the stage together that night.

The rest of the evening was fun—surreal, but fun. Lots of UK appearances made me feel at home. Ed Sheeran, Mumford and Sons, and Elton John all sounded great. It was loud and went on late, and by the time Beth and I got back to the hotel, I could still hear the music and the crowds and the party atmosphere echoing deep inside my head.

I closed my eyes and smiled once more at how such a raw and uncomplicated event in that tiny little chapel had somehow led to all this. I thought about the word *favor* and how the smile of God over our lives can open doors that otherwise would remain firmly shut. I knew this experience was a God-ordained one, and I was glad that my wise and stunning wife had reminded me to savor the moment and find God at work in it.

The next morning I really liked the way it was so quiet in the hotel room. The sun was already up and even out on the balcony the only sounds belonged to the occasional passing cars and the waves pawing at the beach. I skimmed the news. For all the fun and memories laid down the night before, life was still carrying on just the same as it ever had.

There were so many messages of encouragement from friends and family, nice words that made me smile and feel grateful. Lots of other kind messages flowed my way on social media too. But when I opened my emails I came across something that completely stopped me in my tracks. It was a beautifully written message from a woman I'd never met. Reading it was an epiphany, nothing less.

I am writing to you to tell you the story of my Uncle, Charlie Burton. Last May, my Uncle was diagnosed with Lung Cancer at the age of 46 and was given about a 50% chance to live. It threw my entire family for a loop. How could he have cancer? And lung cancer? He didn't even smoke! From the beginning my Uncle turned to God, but it was truly amazing to see how his faith grew through his sickness. Not because of his sickness, but because of his children and their faith in God. He was never mad, scared, or angry about his situation, just sad that there was a possibility that he would not get to experience certain things life has to offer.

At his funeral, my cousin shared about the first time my Uncle heard your song "10,000 Reasons." My Uncle felt like you were speaking to him. He asked my cousin to download it for him and would listen to it often, especially in his darker moments as we continued to find out that his cancer spread from his lungs, to his spine, then to his liver and brain. As we rang in the New Year, my Uncle went into the hospital with back pain and would never come out. All the while his faith remained strong and that strength came from your song.

On January 17th, just two days after my Uncle's 47th birthday, he passed away. As it came time to take him off the ventilator, my cousin asked the nurses if he could play music for my Uncle so he could hear his favorite song as he passed. "10,000 Reasons" filled the room and my Uncle continued to "sing his praises" as he went home to be with God. Your song has become so much more than a song. It helps us to accept the situation because it reminds us that my Uncle was ok with where he was going. As it was played at his funeral, I think all of us could feel his presence there. Every time my cousins hear your song they are reminded of their father, who in his darkest hours, stood by his faith.

This wasn't the first time someone had written in to say that the song had helped them get through a difficult season in life, but it was the first time I'd ever been told of someone having it sung to them as they took their last breaths here on earth. I put my phone down and sat quietly. What little noise there had been before now faded. I felt my breath grow heavy within my lungs. God was close.

The timing of that moving and inspiring email was so poignant. I was hearing God speaking loud and clear to my heart. I didn't get into all this to win awards. I wrote songs to reach the heart of God and refresh the hearts of His children. And I wrote because my own fragile heart needed healing too.

I was just a kid when I first started out in all this, but by that age I had probably experienced more pain and loss than most other kids I knew. At times, singing these simple songs of worship to God was just about the only thing that helped.

> I wrote songs to reach the heart of God and refresh the hearts of His children.

I found out early on that these worship songs we sing are not just about us talking to God. They're a means of Him talking to us too.

That's why I write and sing. I want to use this gift to usher in hope and peace to people's desperate situations. I want to announce the glorious and the eternal over the pattern of our everyday lives.

I went back to that email a few times that day and pictured Charlie Burton lying on a hospital bed, his final moments on earth being played out to a song that speaks of thankfulness, trust, and a never-ending journey with God.

"That's what it's all about," I whispered.

The Grammys night was fun, and I'm grateful to God for the chance to be part of an adventure like that. But it easily takes second place to receiving an email like the one from Charlie's niece. It's no way near as profound as the privilege of singing a song like this in the hospital room of a woman fighting cancer with faith on fire. And it doesn't really compare to the joy of opening a video clip and seeing some amazing schoolkids in Africa singing the song heartily in a dusty township.

The fact is, so much of what we strive for in life is measurable; but are those trophies really the best things we could pursue? Some songwriters or artists chart their success by units sold, number of awards won, or how many people showed up to a concert. It's not the healthiest way to live, but I guess we're all prone to a bit of that.

The stuff I really like is way too deep and too transformational to ever be summed up on a spreadsheet. The email from Charlie Burton's niece fell firmly into that category. It was immeasurable. There was no chart or graph for it. In an unshakable act of faith, Charlie was making this song his sound track as he departed to be with Jesus. How on earth do you attach a value to such a profound and precious moment?

It's the immeasurable stuff like this that really counts. It's those "off the charts" moments when something is so clearly the hand of God at work that no human hand would dare take credit for it.

There's a beach all the way down on the southwest tip of England, in Cornwall, that people call Lego Beach. On any given day, after just a little digging, you'll find a piece of Lego there. It's all thanks to the fact that back in 1997 the container ship *Tokio Express*, bound for New York, was caught up in a storm twenty miles out. A freak wave—the kind only seen once every hundred years—lashed the ship. The *Express* tipped sixty degrees one way, then forty degrees back the other, and the corkscrew motion sent sixty-two shipping containers crashing into the sea. One of them just happened to be filled with Lego pieces. Four million, eight hundred thousand pieces, to be precise.

Humorously, among the usual Lego bricks and yellow figures were lots of nautical-themed pieces: pirate cutlasses, dragons, scuba gear, flippers, and spear guns. Two decades after the event, that brightly colored plastic is still washing up on the shore.[1]

TREASURE HUNTING

Lego Beach reminds me of what it means to adopt an attitude of worship. There's never any shortage of treasure to find, never any lack of reasons to sing out our praises to God. Reminders of His goodness and greatness are washing up on the shoreline of our lives every single day. With our eyes open wide and a little digging around, we'll soon find ourselves with plenty of reasons to worship Him.

From creation to the cross, from the incarnation to the resurrection and ascension, we never have to

> Rhythm of worship: breathing in God's wonders and then breathing out in awe and praise.

invent anything new. Worship is simply a contemplation of who God has already revealed Himself to be and how He has intervened in our lives. It's never about inventing a new story; we're just retelling the precious old story of how God involves Himself in our lives. We remember, and we reply. We recount, and we respond. This is the rhythm of worship: breathing in God's wonders and then breathing out in awe and praise.

Think about those numbers for a moment.

After the *Tokio Express* was hit, it sent 4.8 million bobbing Legos into the water. It was enough to keep washing up on that Cornish shore for decades to come.

Two thousand years after Jesus's birth, death, and resurrection, the goodness of our Lord keeps showing up daily in our lives as well.

If you think about it, "10,000 Reasons" is nothing short of a colossal understatement.

OVERFLOW

I love looking at old hymnbooks. Just skimming down the contents page it's plain to see how these vintage worship songwriters loved to sing about every possible aspect of God.

Take a look at almost any hymnbook and you'll find a list of themes that likely puts some of our more recent efforts to shame. Scan just a couple of pages and you'll find an abundance of the names of God, and so many facets of His nature and character. They're singing of mighty acts and merciful ways. They're speaking of God as Trinity—Father, Son, and Holy Spirit. They're telling

His glorious story from Scripture—the God of yesterday, today, and forever who never fades or falters, and who faithfully works on behalf of His people.

When it comes to singing the worth of God, the reasons are never in short supply. That's why a hymn writer such as Charles Wesley could pen sixty-five hundred poems and hymns or the phenomenal Fanny Crosby could write a thousand or so more.

My favorite hymn of all is just one verse long. It was the last lyric to be uttered by my songwriting hero, Charles Wesley. He was eighty years old and lying on his deathbed, and yet even then he could not stay silent. He reflected on the words of Psalm 73, "Whom have I in heaven but You? And there is none upon earth that I desire besides You. My flesh and my heart fail; but God is the strength of my heart and my portion forever" (vv. 25–26 NKJV).

Physically weak in those final moments, he called his wife to his side and had her transcribe these final lyrics:

> *In age and feebleness extreme,*
> *Who shall a helpless worm redeem?*
> *Jesus, my only hope Thou art,*
> *Strength of my failing flesh and heart:*
> *O could I catch one smile from Thee,*
> *And drop into eternity!*

The mix of poetry and pure devotion is electric. It's obvious how much Wesley knew Christ and how deep an assurance he had that he was about to go and be with his Lord forever. Those last two lines are some of the greatest worship lyrics you could ever read:

O could I catch a smile from Thee,
And drop into eternity!

Isn't that the most amazing way to die? There was such an unshakable hope running through his heart and soul that Wesley wasn't content to be quiet in that moment, to drift away in silence. He still had a song to sing, welling up from the deepest place inside of him.

This final outburst was no mere religious ritual; it was the eruption of his soul in praise. It was the overflow of a fascinated heart. He'd started writing songs at the age of twenty-seven, and even in these very last moments, he still had more to say.

I think my huge admiration for Wesley's last hymn must have been somewhere in the mix when I wrote the lyrics to the last verse of "10,000 Reasons." That part of the song seems to resonate the deepest with people, probably because we all know we will face such a moment. I treasure the thought that even when our bodies are failing and our breath begins to fade, we can still be found with an undying song of devotion in our hearts and on our lips:

Still my soul will
Sing Your praise unending

Can you imagine being like Charles Wesley when you face your final minutes here on earth? Can you imagine being so aware of the goodness and glory of God in that moment that with your last few breaths you have no other option but to continue in praise? Imagine the last strains of your song *here* being the first notes of your song *there*—an uninterrupted melody of eternal worship for our God and King. And imagine that when we get through the first 10,000 reasons of why He is so utterly worthy of our devotion, we'll just be getting started.

10,000 years
And then forevermore

CHAPTER 2

PREACH TO YOURSELF

There were some pretty good reasons for me not to go to church that night. First, I was only seven years old and had school the next day. Then there was the fact that the evening service was being run by some visiting Californians whom nobody knew much about. But the biggest reason of all was that, just one month before, I had sat on those same pews and witnessed the funeral of my father.

His death was a double shock for me, because in addition to finding out that he would no longer be around, I later discovered that he had taken his own life. Knowing a parent has chosen suicide brings up a lot of questions when you're so young. You begin to wonder whether any part of it had to do with you. And your heart can

> Knowing a parent has chosen suicide brings up a lot of questions when you're so young.

wrestle with many other questions too. Didn't he love us enough to stay around? Had I done something terrible to deserve this or make it happen?

Little wonder I remember so few details of my dad's funeral. How could a kid even begin to process something like that? I can remember getting in the funeral car, and I can picture myself at the crematorium. That's about all.

Yet, in contrast, that evening service I attended with my mum and brother just one month later remains the most vivid memory of my entire childhood.

FIRST ENCOUNTER

Ours was the kind of church building that wasn't built to impress. It was designed for participation, for adventure. It was modern, big by British church standards, and though it still had wooden pews, an organ, and a choir stall, everything was bright, informal, and comfortable. The front area beyond the Communion rail was wide and carpeted and designed to offer an open invitation for any and all to come forward. At the end of every service you could see any number of children running and rolling around up there, delighting in the wide open space. At times, the building felt less like a church and more like an all-age playroom.

There weren't many other children walking up the hill to the church that night, but as my mum shepherded us across the busy car park, I knew I wanted to be there. The air outside was still warm from the summer day, and inside it was as if all that warm evening light had poured in through the doors.

We were wedged into the choir stalls, and it gave me a good view of the people preparing to lead the service as well as the congregation. They seemed taller than most adults to me, and they dressed differently. There wasn't a tie or a blazer among them, and when they laughed, their voices were loud and bright.

I wasn't the only one staring. Familiar faces from our church strained to get a better look at what was going on at the front. In what was usually a wide open space were now musical instruments set up on the carpet—a keyboard and guitar, plus a handful of microphone stands.

I didn't need to talk or ask questions or know what was going to happen next. Just staring was enough for me. As they started to play, I couldn't take my eyes off the white-haired, bearded, bearlike guy at the keyboard. He had something about him that was magnetic, something so compelling that it was impossible to ignore.

But the main thing was the sound. The songs were so relaxed and natural—no rigid religious framework or hollow ritual in sight. I was hooked. It all just seemed so real, and way more relevant to my young ears than most of the church music I'd heard up until then.

They played song after song, each one flowing into the other. I was aware of hands being raised and a new kind of warmth in the church, but the only person I really wanted to look at was that big teddy-bear guy sitting at the keyboard. *This has to be the best music I've ever heard*, I thought. Listening to the band play and the whole church sing was like inhaling pure sunshine. I was encountering something I'd never known existed.

I couldn't have wrapped my words around it at that tender age, and years would pass before I could begin to make sense of what happened to me—as well as the rest of the church—that night. Today I'd describe it as the people of God, in the presence of God, pouring out the praises of God. Right there, in that same room where I'd attended my dad's funeral just those few weeks before, I was introduced to one of the most gloriously powerful dynamics on earth: the worshipping church.

I doubt I understood even a fraction of the lyrics. But I loved the experience, as intangible and incomprehensible as it was. I suppose I didn't need to be able to define it or appreciate just how significant this first visit from the Vineyard Movement would become for the church in the UK. All I knew was that within the songs themselves there was something more powerful than I'd ever come across.

I can still remember what it sounded like when I got caught up in my first memorable encounter with the Holy Spirit of God. The songs, gentle yet epic as they were, had been the gateway. They were so simple and so nicely written that it was possible to catch on to them instantly, even if you were a little kid still confused and broken up by grief. Those songs did not put up any barriers, nothing complicated about them that would prevent you from entering in. They were a window onto the ways of God, and a welcome into His heart.

The songs were a window onto the ways of God, and a welcome into His heart.

It was not until a few years later that I started to play guitar and learned how to sing the songs for myself, but on that night in that church service a seed was planted inside of me. I saw how music could affect the soul and how a song could unlock something special in the heart of a worshipper.

REVERENCE AND REFUGE

My guitar-playing journey happened in two distinct stages. I was ten years old when I first gave it a try. My mum found me a guitar and someone who would teach me how to play it. The guitar itself was a classical one that had already been used by plenty of others. The pattern around the sound hole had long since faded, and the body had more chips on it than the hood of our car. But it was mine and I loved it.

The guy I went to for lessons matched my guitar perfectly. He was equally flawed and was showing plenty of signs of being treated a little roughly from time to time. Even at my young age I knew it wasn't quite normal for me to turn up to a lesson and see him with a black eye or a limp. When a knock on the front door interrupted one of our lessons, my teacher looked panicked, handed me a thick wad of cash, and told me to hold on to it while he went and spoke to whoever was calling for him. It was after that particular lesson that I told Mum it was probably time for me to take a break.

Quitting lessons coincided with the guitar exam board letting me know that I would not be allowed to take my grade 2 exam using metal strings, rather than the classical nylon ones. I'd written them a long and probably precocious letter pointing out how old school they were and how much better my steel strings sounded to my ears, but it hadn't worked. So I pinned the letter to the cork notice board in my bedroom as a constant reminder that I fought the law and the law won. Then I put my three-quarter-size guitar back into its worn fake brown leather sleeve and stuffed it on top of my wardrobe. And there it stayed, collecting dust for the next few years. That was stage one.

Stage two came around in my early teenage years. By then I was a full-on follower of Christ, and the worship music I'd first heard at the age of seven was becoming more and more a part of my life. I loved looking out for these new songs and decided that rather than just wait for someone to play them on Sunday at church, I'd have a go myself at home on the weekdays in between. I hated the thought of going all the way from one Sunday to the next without finding some moments to connect with the Father through these songs.

I grabbed that tiny guitar out of its floppy case, gave it a quick dusting down, bought some new (steel) strings, and decided I could teach myself the basics.

> I grabbed that tiny guitar and decided I could teach myself the basics.

At first the tips of my fingers hurt like crazy, making me slightly regret the move away from those more comfortable nylon strings. But I didn't really mind the pain; I just wanted to play the songs. Over and over again.

Before long my fingers toughened up and that guitar never went back in its case. I loved the worship music that surrounded me, but I wasn't just playing these songs for creative reasons. My teenage years became the most turbulent of my life, and these songs of hope and worship were becoming a lifeline. I was thirteen years old, and I was being abused.

After the abuse began, I found myself increasingly drawn to worship. I discovered that not only was the throne room of God a place of reverence, but it was also the ultimate place of refuge. It was my hiding place. Sometimes in that season nothing else seemed to make sense. But somehow this place of worship always did. Even when everything else in my world felt as though it was breaking and shaking apart, even though there was so much instability, a lot of pain, and a lot of confusion, I knew I had one place I could run to.

Worship was a constant in my life, a place where I could "hang out" that wasn't subject to change. It was a place of security and serenity. It was the place where I knew I could find Jesus, ruling and reigning over my life in love and stability. He was the unshakable One, the same yesterday, today, and forever. There with Him, I finally felt as though I could breathe. And though I didn't understand why I was being abused, somehow these worship songs reminded me that I had not been abandoned.

Worship provided me with the chance to quiet the fears and anxieties and instead to focus on God. And it taught me a valuable lesson: even though worship is not *about* us, and it's not primarily *for* us, in the kindness of God's economy, worship *helps* us.

Something happens when we open up our hearts to God in praise. It's as if we give Him a special welcome to work deeply within us and open up His heart to us. Worship isn't just the act of uploading our praise and devotion to God; there's a simultaneous download too. We get a reminder of who God is, a revelation of His grandeur and grace. It's the sort of transfer that enriches our hearts and refreshes our souls. As John Piper once put it, "Worship is a feast of the glorious perfections of God, in Christ."

TALKING BACK

Even though I was thirteen years old and had a lot to fear, I found that worshipping Jesus through music was so healing for me, so freeing. I found out that when we sing our songs, not only do we get to praise God, but we also get to preach to ourselves.

> # I found that worshipping Jesus through music was so healing for me, so freeing.

The great teacher Dr. Martyn Lloyd-Jones once wrote a piece on preaching to yourself that I found very striking. He asked, "Have you realized that most of your unhappiness in life is due to the fact that you are listening to yourself instead of talking to yourself?"[1]

Every one of us always hears someone—or something—talking. Whether it's an external voice or an internal one, we're all constantly on the receiving end of some message or another, especially when life is difficult. But it doesn't have to end there. We can actually dictate the conversation, just as the psalmist did. We can learn to talk back.

"Why, my soul, are you downcast?" the psalmist asked in Psalms 42 and 43. He was feeling depressed, crushed, and defeated. And yet he stood up and chose to speak to himself: "I will remember.… I will yet praise him" (NIV). It was as if he made a deliberate choice to tackle his anxiety and worries head on.

So when we're confused, troubled, disquieted, lonely, or stressed, this is what we need to do: take ourselves in hand, speak to ourselves, and allow God's wisdom to enter in. In this way, our worship can be a weapon, helping us defeat our fears with faith and answer our anxieties with a sense of holy assurance.

King David did it in Scripture. We're told that faced with an immensely pressured situation he "strengthened himself in the LORD" (1 Sam. 30:6 NKJV). Perhaps some of the psalms he penned were part of the process in that moment. When we declare unchanging truth, not only do we honor God with it, but we also help ourselves.

Some say that talking to one's self is the first sign of madness. But in the life of worship, talking to yourself is essential. Remembering and repeating the truths of God in worship can be the very thing that revitalizes your soul. Remember the richness of His grace. Recall that He is the God who is slow to anger and swift in mercy. Retell the story of Calvary to your weakened heart. And just as the psalmist did three thousand years ago, rehearse the fact over and over again that God's love endures forever. And don't stop there—look ahead too. Remind yourself that a glorious future is coming. Choose hope over hopelessness, and faith instead of fear. Talk to yourself; take yourself in hand. Sing the truth over your troubled soul.

I don't know if the seven-year-old me would have liked the song "10,000 Reasons." I like to think I would have, especially as my own kids seem to connect with it now. But in my early years, some important truth was reaching me through those worship songs. I don't think I understood every word I sang, but I know some of it hit home. By the time I reached those stormy teenage years, I was already standing on a firm foundation, and some solid ground. And I'm convinced that those songs of praise, hope, and adoration I kept hearing at church week after week were no small part of that.

I don't know if the seven-year-old me would have liked "10,000 Reasons."

Worship is about what you choose to magnify. It's when we magnify the wrong things that we start to get into trouble. Maybe your bank balance isn't in great shape right now and it's all you can think about when you wake up in the morning. Or perhaps you're walking through some friction in a relationship and you can't seem to see beyond it and focus on anything else in life.

It's so easy to amplify the wrong things. We can so quickly become consumed with these realities, and our hearts and minds become ruled by them. Of course none of them—or any other such examples—are irrelevant. In truth, they are very real issues that can be heavy to carry. But the problem comes when, instead of extolling the glory and goodness of Christ, who rules and reigns over our lives and holds all things together, we magnify these other factors instead.

In worship, we learn to magnify His promises instead of our problems, His track record instead of our trials, and His faithfulness instead of our fears. With the naked eye we can look up at that twinkling night sky and see a star shining away, but it takes a telescope to allow us to see a slightly different, fuller, picture.

In reality, that star is a gigantic burning mass, hotter and more dynamic than we could even begin to imagine; but a telescope allows us to comprehend a little more fully what's really going on. We're not making that star any bigger, but as we zoom in with the magnification of that telescope, we witness a greater degree of the true reality.

That very same dynamic happens in worship. When we magnify the name of Jesus, it's not that we make Him any bigger. His grace and His glory are already completely off the charts of our comprehension, and of course no one could ever add anything to almighty God. But instead, our magnification of Him is an act of getting more deeply in touch with the true reality of His glory and love. We're journeying further into His mercy and majesty, and the eyes of our hearts are beholding a little more of the awesome wonder of who it is we're coming before.

As well as honoring Him, we also benefit from the act of magnifying Jesus. For when we magnify the right things, life looks very different. I always like to say that Jesus is worthy of our worship and He's also worth worshipping. Even if our praise had zero benefit to us, Jesus has revealed more than enough of Himself to be found utterly deserving of our highest and our best. Worship unlocks so much blessing in our lives, much of which I'm sure we don't ever really recognize. The truth is, the activity of worship is good for the soul—we tell God how great He is, but in the process we also tell ourselves that we are known and loved by One so gloriously powerful and graciously kind.

I love it when I meet people who remind me of this dynamic in worship. Especially when they're shorter than me.

"I'M SO BRAVE"

Chase was even smaller than I imagined. But bolder too. Between his Spider-Man T-shirt, Spider-Man sneakers, and cheeky grin, I could tell he was a firecracker. I guess you have to be to have spent over half your life under the threat of relapse and secondary cancers.

Back in 2012, when he was just two and a half, Chase was diagnosed with a brain tumor. It was a rare one that also affected his spinal cord. There was no known cure. His chance of survival was put at less than 20 percent. Even that word *survival* was qualified: doctors said that long-term survival meant living another three to five years. His parents were told that they had two options, maybe three at best. None of them sounded like miracle cures.

So Chase began a run of treatments that would extend for fourteen months. He underwent chemotherapy. He received radiation on his brain. There were surgeries, maybe ten or twelve of them, many because of problems relating to the central line in his chest that fed him throughout the sixteen months when he couldn't eat. He spent so much time in the hospital that whenever the car pulled up outside in preparation for more treatments, tests, or appointments, Chase would call out, "I'm home! I'm home!"

Three years after his diagnosis, I met Chase, his sister, two brothers, and parents a little while before starting worship with a whole bunch of people on the outskirts of Chicago. We joked around a little, and then I heard from his parents about what a remarkable crew of worshippers Chase and his family were. They told me how they sang as they drove into the hospital and how they carried on singing as they waited in preprocedure rooms. They talked about how they'd shared

"10,000 Reasons" with doctors and nurses and even the music thera-pists so they could sing it with Chase whenever they went to his room.

"So often it was the last thing he'd hear at night," said his mom, Ellie. "And on the days Chase was receiving radiation treatment, he would whisper, 'I'm so brave,' as he drifted out of consciousness. In those dark cancer days when the fevers wouldn't break and the cancer cells wouldn't leave, the song wrapped us up as we'd sit beneath it. There were times and seasons when our hearts were broken and we couldn't call out, and the only thing that came from us to God were the words of that song."

It was a privilege to be able to watch Chase and his family as they joined in with all those other wor-shippers that night in Chicago. I could see Chase sing, clap, and raise his arms, and even jump about a little. And when it was time to sing the last song, it was a joy to be able to pause, let the room grow quiet, and share a little of Chase and his family's story.

> "On the days Chase received radiation treatment, he would whisper, 'I'm so brave.'"

It struck me then, as it has so many times, that the church exists so we can carry one another's burdens. It exists to serve God, to praise Him, and to be His hands and feet out in the world. It also exists to stand alongside a young family who is faithfully working their way through a challenge that many would consider a nightmare. And yet still they praised, still they sang.

So we sang the song to God that night, and we sang it with Chase too. We sang it hoping that God would continue to download

His peace and love to that family through the song, and we sang it knowing He could do the same for us.

Seeing Chase and the others sing it so boldly that evening told me loud and clear that here was a family intent on magnifying the right thing. They were making it through the turbulence of this storm with their hearts of worship intact. And as I write this several months after meeting Chase, I'm pleased to say that's exactly what they're still doing today—still trusting and leaning on God as they walk the long road together.

HE GIVES AND TAKES AWAY

A few years ago, on a trip to the United States, I woke up to a devastating report on the national news. A friend and fellow worship leader's young daughter Maria Sue had died in a horrible accident on the driveway at home.

I sent a message of love and support but of course didn't expect to hear back anytime soon. Then a couple of days later I was sitting on an airport shuttle, about to make the trip back from America to England, and I saw Steven's name flash up on my phone. I couldn't believe he would call, and I was almost scared to answer it.

"Steven?"

"Hey, Matt."

"Oh, Steven, I'm so sorry to hear about Maria. You can't imagine how many people are praying for you and the family right now. I guess none of us really have the right words to say right now, but I want you to know we love you and we're thinking of you all constantly."

"Thank you, Matt; that means so much. I have a request. Is there any chance you're in America right now? Mary Beth and I were pondering the memorial service, and we wondered if there was any way you could join us tomorrow in Nashville and lead your song 'Blessed Be Your Name.'"

One line from the song played loud in my mind: "You give and take away." I knew it was a brave and bold choice for them to sing this. It struck me as evidence of who they were as a family—that even in the midst of all their pain and grief, they would choose to put a marker in the ground and sing those costly words. Most times our lyrics don't cost much to sing. But I realized there would be a huge weight of faith for them to sing a lyric like this at a time like that.

The next day, I stood up to sing in that huge and packed-out church building. There on the front row were Steven, Mary Beth, and the rest of their family. It was hard to get the words out, but ultimately it wasn't me leading the worship in that service. It was them. I was just accompanying them on guitar as they stood there setting an example of worship, trust, and sacrifice for all to see.

> Even in the midst of all their pain and grief, they chose to sing those costly words.

Every single person there that day knew the Chapmans had lost their adopted daughter in the most horrible of circumstances. And no doubt every single person was moved by how they were still standing, and still singing, at a time like this.

Songs of faith and worship can be a gift—a window onto the heart of God and a weapon of truth to use in the darkest night. They can reach us when we're overwhelmed, when no logic, no words of comfort, and no rational explanation can ever really seem to help. They can be a gift when we're grieving, when we're facing unanswerable questions, or when we're sitting in the doctor's office listening to the word *cancer* being used to describe the reason for the failing health of a precious child.

They can become a bridge between the pain and uncertainty of this world and the compassion and steadfastness of God Himself. They can help bring us into His presence, a place where we stand reassured that nothing but God and His love can overwhelm us.

They remind us of the unchanging truths that can sustain us, no matter how hard the problem and no matter how weary we have become from all the holding on. They remind us that God is closer than we know even when life is stained by grief. They remind us that she's safe in the arms of Jesus, even though our hands are empty. And they can remind us that no matter what trials we may face, we can still choose to bless the Lord. No matter what.

CHAPTER 3

SONGS IN THE NIGHT

In the world of nature, you only really find out whether a tree is evergreen when the season turns to winter. Throughout all the other seasons, to the untrained eye, it can be hard to tell the difference between those trees that will eventually shed their leaves and those that will keep them. Yet once the sun fails to climb quite as high in the sky and the temperature drops, the truth begins to emerge. When winter sets in, it soon becomes clear which trees have kept hold of their leaves and which have not.

And so it is too in the spiritual life. As worshippers, perhaps we don't really know what we're made of until we encounter a little winter in our lives. When things are at their toughest, when life feels at its most frail, that's when we really find out what kind of worshippers we are.

Can we remain evergreen followers of Christ, still able to bring a song of praise in the deep dark of winter? Anyone can sing during the daytime, when life is all brightness and ease. When there's peace and prosperity, when the people we love are healthy and the plans we have made look as though they're in line with God's will, it's not so hard to raise a hand and utter a thank-you. But can we still find our way to the place of praise when the sun goes down? Can we offer up a song in the night?

Perhaps we don't really know what we're made of until we encounter a little winter in our lives.

That's a phrase that comes up several times in Scripture. The book of Job talks about the God who "gives songs in the night" (35:10 NIV). We can see it in action too in the story of Paul and Silas (Acts 16:16–40). There they were in jail; it was midnight. Their hands and feet were bound in the stocks and they'd been treated unfairly. In the darkness of that prison most of our hearts would perhaps give way to fear, discouragement, or dejection. But not Paul and Silas. Their bodies might have been chained up, but their spirits were free. And what were they doing? Singing. From their lips came songs of worship, trust, and praise. And that praise became their sound track for a miraculous release from prison.

Then there's Jesus at the end of the Last Supper (Matt. 26:17–30). As He celebrated the Passover meal with His disciples, we're told that they sang a final hymn. Most likely the song they chose was the "Great Hallel," Psalm 136. Imagine Christ standing there, His final hours already counting down, and He adds His voice to the others as they sing over and over again, "His love endures forever … His love endures forever … His love endures forever" (NIV).

In full knowledge of what was soon to come, and with the shadow of the cross falling over Him, Jesus chose to sing with His disciples this song of praise. Facing toward Gethsemane and headed toward Golgotha, and yet the Son of God sang of goodness and love.

THE NIGHTINGALE

Of all the birds that fill the skies, there aren't many that continue to sing at night. Owls will hunt and call out to others, and robins, blackbirds, song thrushes, and mockingbirds can all be heard from time to time. But of the handful of species that continue to sing after sunset, it is the nightingale that stands out most. They're the ones that consistently keep on singing when the darkness descends.

Can we somehow do the same, when the darkness creeps up on our own lives? Can we keep singing even when it grows so gloomy that we can barely see our hand in front of our face? Can we find within ourselves a song of praise that doesn't depend on our present circumstances but is fueled by an unfading hope in the name of God? Can we still trust that there's more of our story to be written and believe deep down that whatever opposition we're facing right now, our God is still very much in control?

Whatever may pass
And whatever lies before me
Let me be singing
When the evening comes

The question is the same for every worshipper: Can we still find our way to the place of praise in spite of the darkness? Can we still rise up and bring to Him a song in the night? I was reading the *London Times* when I first heard about the men who were shot and killed as they sang the song. I read about their arrest, their years in prison on Bali, their journey to faith, and their eventual execution by firing squad. It was not a long article, but I was intrigued to know more, and amazed that "10,000 Reasons" had found its way to them.

It took several months until I was able to get the full story. I finally heard it told by Australian pastor Christie Buckingham, who had known some of the men well and walked with them as their faith went from strength to strength over their final three years. When I read about these condemned men as they faced their final moments on earth, *remarkable* seemed like too weak a word to use. Here is the story, told by the pastor who lived through the experience:

> ## Can we still find our way to the place of praise in spite of the darkness?

Pastor Christie was unimpressed when she first heard about Andrew Chan and Myuran Sukumaran. She read about their arrest for attempting to smuggle heroin out of Indonesia. "How dumb can you be and still breathe?" she wrote in her prayer journal. "Nevertheless, Lord, show Your mercy."

Of course, she had no idea that the Lord would use her so directly as He answered her prayer.

Six years into Andrew and Myu's sentence, Pastor Christie was at a conference on Bali. A friend told her that she knew the two men. "I've told them you're in town. They'd love it if you could visit them in prison and pray for them."

Pastor Christie remembered the scripture about visiting those in prison. She knew that going to see them was the least she could do.

Overcrowded and run down, Kerobokan Prison held twelve hundred inmates convicted of everything from drug smuggling to terrorist bombings. It was an intimidating place, and neither Pastor Christie nor her husband had any idea what was awaiting them inside the infamous jail. Yet as they sat on the ground in a wide courtyard, they found that Andrew and Myu did not match her image of two convicted drugs traffickers. Together they talked about what life was like inside the jail and how their faith was holding up.

"I feel like I am freer inside these walls than most people are outside them," said Andrew. "I don't have all those distractions and choices that you have. Every day I am awakened at 7:00 a.m., and every evening I'm locked up at 5:30 p.m. I don't get to choose what I eat, and I don't get to choose who comes to visit. The only choices I really get to make are how I react to things.

Andrew and Myu did not match her image of two convicted drugs traffickers.

The only power I've got is how I deal with this. So I'm freer, you see?"

Pastor Christie listened as Andrew spoke. She thought about the questions she had been asking of her own faith: How would she hold up if she were imprisoned with no control over the basic events of life? There, sitting on the ground in front of her, locked within rough prison walls, was a perfect example of how to live life with God fully at the center.

Myu explained how Andrew used to drive him crazy by talking about God. Gradually, though, the faith that had irritated him began to intrigue him, and soon he too had rediscovered his faith in Jesus. Since that day, both men had dedicated their lives to demonstrating God's love to others within the jail.

When it came time to leave, Pastor Christie told them they were both remarkable. "If there's anything I can do to help, will you let me know?"

Two weeks later, she received a letter at home in Melbourne, Australia, and noticed the Indonesian stamp. It was Andrew, writing with a long list of items for which he was seeking assistance. Like Myu, he knew he'd never walk out of prison, even if he were granted clemency from his death sentence. He knew that the rest of his life—however short or long—was to be lived out behind bars. But he and Myu knew that other inmates would walk out, and both men wanted to do all they could to rehabilitate these prisoners. They wanted to make sure that other prisoners didn't reoffend and that they would receive training while in Kerobokan so they could get a decent job upon release. All Myu and Andrew wanted was the chance to secure the freedom of others, not themselves.

All Myu and Andrew wanted was to secure the freedom of others, not themselves.

And so began a friendship that lasted for years. Pastor Christie campaigned on their behalf and visited when she could, while Andrew and Myu continued to pastor and train fellow inmates.

"Mrs. B," said Andrew one day as Pastor Christie sat on the familiar dirt opposite him, "you will not believe it."

"What's wrong? You seem like you're ruffled."

"Well, there's a guy who hasn't turned up to his English class three times in a row. I found him and asked him what was going on. He said, 'You don't know how I feel. I've got ten years in this place.' I said, 'Look me in the eye and tell me that once more. I dream of having just ten years in this place.' So the guy picked up his pencils and went off to his lesson. Can you believe he said that to me? Can you believe it?"

Months turned into years, and still the Indonesian government showed no sign of lifting the death sentences. Three years after Pastor Christie first met them, Andrew and Myu were transferred under armed guard to another prison on an island a short distance off the coast of Java. It was called Nusakambangan, but most people knew it by another name: Execution Island.

Pastor Christie watched both men as they prepared for the worst but still believed for the best. She encouraged them to make sure they held no unforgiveness of any kind in their hearts, and she watched them learn how to live with the knowledge that at any point the authorities could announce the seventy-two-hour countdown to their executions.

"Every day above ground is a good day," said Myu more than once.

She encouraged Myu to think of two or three things he was grateful for each day. She knew it would be hard. She'd sat with plenty of people back home in Australia who struggled to name even one or two good things in their lives. But even though life was a dreary routine played out beneath the fear of imminent death, something about Myu's attitude told her that he would be able to do it.

With the move to Execution Island came an increased attempt to get the sentences changed. Pastor Christie had taken some of her teenage daughter's school friends to visit Andrew and Myu. Though they were precisely the age when teens start dabbling in drugs, the visit put them off for life.

Along with others, Pastor Christie told people that it all seemed such a terrible waste, but nothing changed. She and other advocates argued that keeping Myu and Andrew alive and in jail for the rest of their lives would help so many others, but the authorities showed no sign of changing their minds. The Indonesian government was reluctant to back down, fearing that doing so would make them appear weak on drugs.

One Friday in April 2015, Pastor Christie received a call from one of the family members. "Get on a plane," they said. "They're being executed on Tuesday."

Each condemned man was allowed to ask for a spiritual adviser to be with him in his final moments. While Andrew asked his childhood church leader, Myu asked Pastor Christie. A day after the phone call, Pastor Christie arrived in Indonesia and embarked on the long journey to join the other spiritual directors

> "Get on a plane. They're being executed on Tuesday."

and lawyers before making the short boat ride across to Execution Island. By the time the group finally arrived, Myu and Andrew had just a few hours left to live.

As soon as they were ashore, Pastor Christie was shown into a dingy cell with cracked white tiles where Myu was being kept alone. It was hot and humid, and mosquitoes hovered in the air.

"I've been doing those things you said, writing down every day ten things that I'm grateful for," said Myu.

"Ten things?"

"Yes, absolutely." He smiled.

They spent an hour and a half talking about what was coming next. "I want to do this really well," said Myu. "How do I do it?"

Pastor Christie thought for a moment. "The Bible says about entering His courts with thanksgiving and entering His gates with praise."

"Fantastic!" said Myu. "I know exactly what I want to be singing."

Though she could guess what song he was thinking of, she asked him to name it anyway.

"'10,000 Reasons.'"

SACRED PLACE

They'd been singing "10,000 Reasons" for a few months, belting it out every day during Communion. Myu had been brought up a Christian and then wandered away from his faith. Since being imprisoned, much of his knowledge of Scripture he had learned as a child was coming back to him. Bit by bit, his faith returned, just as if he were unpacking a box of old treasures he had long thought lost forever. At times, he felt as though there were so many more than 10,000 reasons to bless the Lord. From the moment he first heard the song, it resonated deeply with him.

Eventually it was time to go. Once outside, Myu paused and looked up. "This is magnificent." He smiled, his eyes transfixed on the night sky. For ten years he had not seen a sunset, a sunrise, or the stars.

"Thank You, Lord; thank You, God, for these stars."

Pastor Christie was escorted from the cell and taken with the other eight spiritual advisers to wait in a tent near the execution spot. As the minutes passed, she remembered how, before she had arrived on the island, she had wondered whether Myu would have a lot of fear or anxiety to cope with. But at that moment it felt as though the whole world was carrying them in prayer. As she waited, she knew that instead of being in a place of slaughter, she was in a sacred place. A place of horror was about to become a holy place.

It was the sound of metal on metal that broke the silence. Pastor Christie couldn't make it out at first but soon realized what it was: the men had been shackled. Like slaves from a bygone age, they shuffled forward out of the darkness, their hands and feet held tight.

A place of horror was about to become a holy place.

Suddenly, out of the darkness, she heard a voice she had grown to know so well over the previous years. It was Andrew's. He was singing a song she knew:

My God is mighty to save,
He is mighty to save.

He paused. "Come on, boys," he said. "We can sing better than this."

Slowly—quietly at first—other voices joined in. With each step and each line of the melody, the song grew louder. *This is such a gift,* Pastor Christie thought as she watched each prisoner grow in courage as they sang. They carried on walking, the sound of the chains and the singing getting louder as they approached. And when they finished their first verse, Pastor Christie and the rest of the spiritual advisers sang the next verse back to them.

Eventually the song ended, and as everyone started to sing "Amazing Grace," the advisers were finally released from the tent to join the men as they approached the clearing.

At first it was just one guard who was crying, then others started sobbing. A line of forty masked guards made a guard of honor as the prisoners shuffled forward toward them. One guard broke ranks and hugged Myu. Another pulled down his mask and said, "Please forgive us. Forgive Indonesia."

"I forgive you," Myu said. Then, looking at each one in turn, he repeated the same words. "I forgive you. I forgive you. I forgive you." Some he thanked too.

The execution site was just a small clearing in the forest. Wooden posts stuck up out of the ground like ragged flagpoles. The guards tied the men to the poles, their elbows bound behind their backs, while the others carried on singing.

"Three minutes," a guard said.

Pastor Christie stood close by Myu. He turned to her. "I'm so sorry to ask you to do this," he said. "But someone has to speak up, and I know that you will. I've chosen you because I know you hate the death penalty and you are not afraid."

"I'll speak up. You can be sure of that, Myu." She paused for a few seconds. "Myu, it's my greatest privilege to be here with you, and a great honor."

With Myu still smiling, they talked a little about how to die well. Soon a soldier tapped her on the shoulder and she knew she had to go. She noticed a narrow green light on his body. She looked back and saw twelve other soldiers approaching. She lifted her arm in front of Myu, not wanting him to see.

"Now, Myu, is there anything you want to say?"

"Yes, I want to forgive these people that are tying me."

"Anything else?"

"Yes, I want to declare God's blessing on Indonesia."

"And is there anything else?"

"Yes, Lord Jesus, I trust You. I trust You, Jesus."

"Okay. The time has come. Let's start singing."

A soldier tapped her on the arm. "One minute," she said. "One minute."

"Myu," she said, "remember what the Lord has said to you."

"I do."

"You have forgiven these people, Myu."

"Yes, I've forgiven them." And then he started to sing:

Bless the Lord O my soul ...
Worship His holy name

Pastor Christie joined in, her voice small in the night. She felt the soldier tug at her arm again and looked around to see that she was the only one still there. "Myu, I'm just going to take a step back. Are you okay?"

"Yes."

She stepped back. "Keep singing, Myu. I'll see you on the other side."

"I'll see you on the other side."

Andrew called her over. She put her hand on his heart. "I thank you for being God's man."

"You keep being God's woman, Mrs. B. Love you."

She walked to the side to join the other spiritual advisers. She could see the green lights had returned. They were lined up on his heart. A plastic sheet was pulled down to keep the advisers out of the line of fire.

Together with Andrew and one of the other prisoners, Myu sang. His voice was loud, not timid in any way. Her mind lingered on specific lines of the song:

> *Whatever may pass*
> *And whatever lies before me*
> *Let me be singing*
> *When the evening comes*

She and Myu had sung it so many times in the previous months, knowing full well that at some point, sooner or later, the evening would come. Now it was finally here, and he was doing exactly what he said he would do; he was singing out praise with his very last breaths.

"Love you, Myu. I'll see you on the other side."
And still they carried on singing.

Your name is great
And Your heart is kind

Then the night was ripped apart as a hundred bullets tore the air.

Silence. Pastor Christie listened intently. She wanted to know for sure that they had died instantly. If they hadn't, Indonesian law stated that they would be left for up to ten minutes before she would have to go and witness them being shot in the head.

"Please let them have gone, Lord," she prayed. "Please."

No noise.

Where there had been singing, now there was nothing. A silence so heavy it was as if it had taken all the light with it.

Somehow, the atmosphere was not what she had expected. She didn't cry or fall to pieces. Instead, the whole place seemed to be filled with a spirit of love. A horrible, tragic occurrence was now a moment of honor, love, and holiness.

She was fully aware of all the prayer, encouragement, and support that came from so many different people in so many different places. A number of people had helped the boys over the years, making them into who they were, and Pastor Christie felt honored to had played a part in the big picture of their lives.

A horrible, tragic occurrence was now a moment of honor, love, and holiness.

A couple of weeks later people flocked to the funerals of Andrew and Myu back in Australia. Andrew's wife spoke of how they had sung "10,000 Reasons" on their wedding day while he was in prison, knowing full well that Andrew's death sentence would be carried out soon. She told people that even though he hated wearing his glasses, Andrew chose to wear them on the night he was killed just so he could look the executioners in the eyes. And she remembered the words he had uttered when he found out that he was to be executed the following week: "Don't worry. Look to Jesus. Look to Jesus."

Upon hearing the story of Myu and Andrew, it struck me that there couldn't be many other examples of worship quite as poignant as this. Their act of devotion led me, and so many others around the world, in the worship of Jesus. And as for their singing, I doubt if there was ever a more powerful version of that song. Their act of worship teaches us that if you can face a firing squad and still be found with a song of worship in your heart and on your lips, then you can pretty much face anything in this life and still be found singing.

And of course, above all, their story reminds us that God is not absent, even when we find ourselves in the darkest of nights.

The dark night of the soul closes in on all of us at one time or another. And when it does, we're faced with a choice. Will we join Paul and Silas and Andrew and Myu as they sing their hearts out to Jesus in the shadows? God is looking for the kind of worshipper who, just like the nightingale, knows how to bring Him a song in the night.

CHAPTER 4

SOUND TRACK FOR THE SOUL

"You coming to swim, Matt?"

I didn't look up. The sound I directed back toward my brother barely registered as a word. My meaning was perfectly clear, though. I was staying right where I was, no matter how inviting the pool outside.

Mum had taken all five of us kids on holiday to Portugal. She said we needed to get away. After the previous twelve months or so, we all knew what she meant. Once the police had found out what was happening to me, the perpetrator eventually ended up in jail. Even though I knew he was locked up back in the UK, being a thousand miles away definitely helped.

The weather was hot and the villa had a pool, but I had barely stepped outside all week. Instead, I chose to stay inside where the air was cooler and there were fewer distractions. After all, my head was full of thoughts and I needed all the peace and quiet I could get.

I was fifteen at the time, but this was not your typical teenage rebellion. In fact, it wasn't a rebellion at all—at least, not the sort that any parent should have to worry about. All I knew for sure was that something deep was happening to me and I wanted—needed—to be alone for a while.

It had all started a couple of weeks earlier. Along with almost everyone else from my church, I'd attended a big Christian conference at a converted agricultural show ground, set up by the leaders of my home church. They happened to be two of the kindest and bravest Christians I'd ever met. One of my key memories soon after losing my father was Pastor Barry taking me along to the local amusement park and treating me to all the rides and cotton candy a seven-year-old kid could ever want. I know it must have meant a lot to me at the time because I can still remember it now.

And Bishop David had shown up in so many of the most intense moments in my life—he christened me and all my siblings, he conducted my dad's funeral service, and then later on in life he married Beth and me and baptized all five of our kids.

In 1989, David and Barry rented a festival site, put the word out wide, and hosted three thousand people at this brand-new Christian family conference. I loved everything about that week— the burger vans, the camping, and chatting late into the night with my youth group mates. And then, of course, there were the worship sessions. I loved the way the meetings flowed from one to another, the air heavy with that same sense of God's presence I'd first tasted all those years before.

On the last night of the gathering, I knew for sure something inside of me had changed. It was the most passionate time of worship I'd ever been a part of. Even now I can hear those thousands of voices in unison singing "Unto the King" in that huge hall that acted like a giant reverb chamber.

David and Barry decided to invite people forward who knew they were called to be worship leaders, singers, and musicians. By personality I was usually the guy in the back row observing cautiously and weighing up everything before jumping in. But not this time. Straightaway I knew I needed to be part of this moment.

I traveled from the back to the front of that huge converted cattle shed as fast as I possibly could. Standing there, I opened up my heart to receive from God. Immediately I felt the weighty closeness of the Holy Spirit in a way I'd never experienced before. I sensed a small group of people praying around me, and I heard their odd phrases as they spoke affirming words over my life and prayed for me to flourish as a worship leader and songwriter.

Most of all, I just sensed God. It was a moment of deep encounter with the Holy One of heaven. And it was a "here am I, send me" moment, as I told Him once again that I was ready to do whatever He put my hand to in life. When I left and walked back to my tent, I knew that whatever had just taken place was a life-changing experience for me.

> **I felt the weighty closeness of the Holy Spirit in a way I'd never experienced.**

THE PSALMS

I didn't dream of new songs that night or wake up the next day suddenly able to play the guitar better than I had before. But by the time we got to Portugal the following week, I could tell that something had shifted. Usually I would have been in the pool with everyone else the whole time, but not now.

I spent some great moments with my family, having all the usual fun and banter and arguments, but instead of swimming and playing in the sun all afternoon, I wanted nothing more than to be alone inside the villa. Here it was quiet and I could devote all my attention to a new passion for worship leading and songwriting that was rising within me. For hours I'd sit on the terra-cotta tiled floor by the window, my Bible open on my lap, my big notebook in hand, and study the Psalms.

I'd read enough of them in the past to know they were special. I had figured out they were the songbooks at the heart of the Bible, and as a kid I always found them the easiest part of Scripture to read. But since being prayed for, something new had happened.

All day long I was thinking about songwriting ideas or coming up with ways to musically link from one song to another in worship. And I'd become pretty much obsessed with the Psalms. I'd read maybe fifty a day, writing notes as I went, highlighting the lines I thought could be good lyrics for songs and making a note of any word or phrase that inspired me.

> I was hungry for God and His glory, and only those 150 psalms seemed to satisfy.

For the whole vacation I was like this, waking up each morning excited about what I was going to learn that day. I was hungry for God and His glory in a way I'd never experienced before—and only those 150 psalms packed into the middle of the Bible seemed to satisfy.

Throughout the whole of my teenage years, and especially in those turbulent early ones, Psalm 121 was my life song. These beautiful words were a constant source of help to me:

> I lift up my eyes to the mountains—
>   where does my help come from?
> My help comes from the LORD,
>   the Maker of heaven and earth.
>
> He will not let your foot slip—
>   he who watches over you will not slumber;
> indeed, he who watches over Israel
>   will neither slumber nor sleep.
>
> The LORD watches over you—
>   the LORD is your shade at your right hand;
> the sun will not harm you by day,
>   nor the moon by night.
>
> The LORD will keep you from all harm—
>   he will watch over your life;
> the LORD will watch over your coming and going
>   both now and forevermore. (NIV)

I remember going to bed crying my eyes out several times during the toughest moments of my teen years, praying myself to sleep with this psalm. I don't know how many times I recited it—it could have been hundreds—but every time I did, I held on to the promise that "He will not let your foot slip" as if the words had been written just for me. I found it amazing that this simple heart cry from a worshipper three thousand years ago could resound so deeply within my own heart too.

The more I studied the Psalms, the more I realized that book has something for everyone—a song for every season of the soul, be it joy or pain, celebration or suffering. I also became aware of just how raw the Psalms are. There were times I'd put my Bible down, sit back against the wall, and stare outside, wondering whether it really was okay to talk to God with such brutal honesty. Occasionally I wondered whether David and the other writers might have gone too far, but all the evidence suggested that God could handle it.

I didn't know it at the time, but I was beginning to form an opinion about what I thought a powerful worship song looked like—and that to connect deeply with people's hearts, a song should have a sense of transparency. Even today I still hold on to that same belief that worship songs must never be just a cerebral affair; their sound needs to express the passionate overflow of an honest heart.

I remember Bono once saying in an interview that when it comes to songwriting, you can have a thousand ideas, but without emotion it's just an essay. Check through the Psalms, and each writer never sounds bored about life—whether it's thanksgiving and dancing, or intercession and lament, the Psalms always sound honest, intense, and passionate. And yet for all this explosive expression, the key thing in the Psalms is that even when they are raw, they are still reverent. Our songs today need that very same mix. Cry out to God, yes, but never forget whom it is you are standing before.

I noticed in the Psalms how often the worshippers moved from desperate requests to deep praise in an instant. Even when they were raging about their circumstances, they were still acknowledging the holiness of God's name and the power of His hand. Because why cry out in His direction unless you believe He has the power to do something about the situation? However pressured or unhappy they might have sounded at times, the psalmists' songs were essentially cries acknowledging that God alone had the heart and the power to intervene in their situations. Raw, yes. But always reverent.

> Bono once said that in songwriting you can have a thousand ideas, but without emotion it's just an essay.

LEARNING TO WRITE

My own private Psalms school carried on for the rest of the summer vacation and beyond. For two months or so, I think the Psalms were all I read. Nothing else had the power to speak to me like they did. And the more I filled myself up with them, the more I wanted to start writing my own responses to God. I didn't know how to read music or write songs, but I just made up my mind to start by dissecting the Psalms—which of course would have been the hymnbook of Jesus as He walked the earth—and then I'd figure out how to do it from there.

God brought some great people into my life to encourage me along the way. My youth leader, Mike, was even more fascinated with worship music than I was, and we'd have huge, long discussions about what worship was and how best to lead it through music in this generation.

> I didn't know how to read music or write songs, but I just made up my mind to start by dissecting the Psalms.

Mike, in his incredible generosity, also took me to London every few weeks to meet with a man named Bryn, who happened to be one of the best guitarists in the country, as well as having a huge heart for worship.

Bryn was also one of the most patient people I'd ever met. I must have driven him nuts, not only because my fingers were some of the least flexible to have ever encountered a fret board, but also by my constant questions about everything to do with guitars, worship, songwriting, and music. I don't think we ever paid Bryn a dime either. He was just being who God had made him to be—a kind and wise mentor with the heart of a shepherd.

When I'd write, I'd sit on my bed surrounded by scraps of paper and sing my two- or three-chord songs. They were all super simple, at first nothing much more than a single expression of devotion and trust. I'd just loop that around, over and over, until I thought of something else to say. Some of the songs were full of thanks and praise. Some of them called on the name and the presence of God.

In others I'd pour out my pain and ask my Father to meet me in my brokenness. Even though none of them ever made it out of my bedroom, it was a great way for me to process some of what I'd walked through in my life. In all of this outpouring of music, I was able to journal my walk with God and try to convey exactly what I wanted to say to Him. And all the while, I was flexing my imagination muscle and learning to write songs.

It always amazes me that we can find new ways of singing to God and we never run out of things to say. Think about that for a moment—not just the few hundred worship songs you've heard in your church or on a record. But consider the heritage of the singing saints. We have two thousand years of musical history, twenty centuries' worth of people pouring out their hearts to God through their poetic and melodic compositions. And yet the well never runs dry.

Essentially there's never anything new to say because we're working from the revelation of God as described in Scripture, but there's always a new way to say it. There's always a fresh angle from which to approach the cross lyrically or a new creative approach to voicing our praise for His splendor.

We have twenty centuries' worth of compositions, and yet the well never runs dry.

An old pop music producer once lightheartedly said that in his genre of music it was only possible to write four kinds of song:

> I love you.
> I hate you.
> Go away.
> Come back!

I love his cheeky insight. But the fact is, when it comes to the worship of our God, there's an amazing spectrum of themes to get our hearts into—just so many shades and colors of His glory and grace. And when we sing about these things, we're rehearsing the reasons why He should be worshipped and reminding ourselves of truth that will help us stand.

That's what the Psalms were doing for me back then, and when I feed on them today, the benefit is no less powerful.

Worshipping God with a heart of trust will change your life. Maybe you're in a storm right now. I can't promise you that the storm will pass immediately; although, of course we pray it will. But I think I can promise you that even if your circumstances don't change straight-away, something inside of you *will*. When we lift our eyes in worship, our perspective shifts. Everything looks a bit different in the light of a glorious God who reigns in love, wisdom, and power over us.

Worship can help us gain a clearer sense of the big picture. When we worship, we let the throne set the tone—not our finances, our struggles, or our worst fears. The more we focus on God and who He is, the more we start to see the whole of our lives through that lens. We let the revelation of who Jesus is dictate the terms; we invite the glory of God to define our story.

In the middle of one of life's storms, you're unlikely to feel like worshipping, let alone finding reasons for thanks and praise. But that is the discipline of worship, and worship is a choice we can always make.

I look back now on my story and I see that the decisions to trust and worship Christ in the toughest and most disorientating moments of my life were actually the smartest choices I ever made. Not only did they give glory to God, but as it turned out, they were good for me too.

TIME TO SING

Recently I came across a young guy named Reuben Hill. I'd seen his story all over the BBC news one day, and it was showing up around the world on social media. Reuben was a fit, healthy man in his early twenties. He was a member of the judo squad and the choir at Imperial College in London, where he was studying for a PhD in physics. One day, with absolutely no warning, he collapsed in his bedroom. After a series of tests and scans, he was told he had a tumor the size of a golf ball growing in the part of his brain responsible for language and communication.

The plan was simple, but also highly experimental. The doctors wanted to use a brand-new procedure in which they would bounce light off brain tissue to determine which cells were normal and which were cancerous. Coincidentally, Reuben was very familiar with these new advances in physics: in his studies he had been working with some of the very same laser technology they were proposing to use.

So on the one hand, he was nervous about having his brain operated on using such a new procedure. This was especially true as the areas in question were very close to his speech and cognition centers, and any wrong move could affect them.

But on the other hand, as he told the man from the BBC, "My inner scientist is fascinated by what they are going to do." He was captivated by the fact that they could point the beam of laser light right onto his exposed brain and then, measuring the frequency of the vibrations, be able to distinguish healthy cells from cancerous ones and remove whatever needed to go.

And so they went to work. It all seemed to be going well, but when the last of the tumor had been removed, it was time to check that those cognition and speech areas hadn't been affected. So they woke up Reuben right there on the operating table and got him talking and singing. He was tired and groggy, but when they asked him to sing one last time, his response was spontaneous.

You can hear it for yourself if you search online. Reuben's voice is deep and slightly croaky, but from it flow these words:

> *The sun comes up*
> *It's a new day dawning*
> *It's time to sing Your song again*
> *Whatever may pass*
> *And whatever lies before me*
> *Let me be singing*
> *When the evening comes*

And he doesn't stop there:

> *Bless the Lord O my soul*
> *O my soul*
> *Worship His holy name*

I had the privilege of meeting Reuben a little while later. I wanted the chance to tell him how inspired I'd been when I watched him on the news. I heard from so many people around the globe who'd also seen his video and were inspired by his resolve to worship—with his brain open, right there on that operating table.

I asked him why he'd started up that particular song. He could have chosen anything. He could have picked a nursery rhyme or some radio song he'd heard a couple of days before. Maybe something with fewer words. But he told me that he'd decided beforehand that if they asked him to test his cognition and speech facilities in this way, then he would sing a song of thanks, trust, and praise. And there it is again: he had *decided*.

Yes, sometimes worship is a spontaneous overflow. But very often it's a decision. It's the choice we make that, come what may, we will be found with a song of thanks and praise in our hearts and on our lips. So in that intense moment, with those BBC news cameras rolling, Reuben chose to sing his song of faith, and his song went all around the world. When I got to meet him, he'd come to one of our worship tour nights in the UK. He explained how he'd have to stand at the back of the venue, away from the bright lights, because he was still prone to epilepsy after his ordeal. So I couldn't really see him joining in "10,000 Reasons" with us that night. But something tells me he was one of the loudest in the room.

> Sometimes worship is a spontaneous overflow. But very often it's a decision.

I love that in moments such as the one in Reuben's operating theater, a simple song like "10,000 Reasons" can become the sound track for the soul. It's obvious that God has ordained music as part of His blessing and presence in this world, and whether it's an age-old psalm or a brand-new composition, these songs can show up in our lives and accompany both our brightest moments and our toughest moments.

CHAPTER 5

GLORIOUSLY DEPENDENT

My good friends Jonas and George and I felt a little self-conscious as we stood in the hospital corridor and put on our yellow gowns, gloves, and face masks. We were grateful, though, and we knew it was a privilege to leave the tour bus outside in the parking lot and make this special visit. We'd walked through the beautiful hospital gardens on that bright California morning talking about how we sensed the hand of God was in this moment. But none of us could have guessed quite how amazing the woman waiting for us on the other side of the doors was.

Mollie Warner had sent a message a few days earlier. She asked if we could sing my song "You Alone Can Rescue" at our worship night in Irvine, in Southern California. She said her husband and daughter would be there, though she could not. She'd be in the hospital.

In the days leading up to the visit, Mollie told us a little more about herself. She was forty-one, married to a worship leader, and had a thirteen-year-old daughter and a ten-year-old son. A few weeks earlier she had been diagnosed with acute myeloid leukemia, the most aggressive form of leukemia there is. The doctors had told her that she was 90 percent affected and that when she first showed up at the hospital, she didn't have much time left. They said she was walking death.

From the moment the door closed behind us, it was clear that this was unlike any hospital room I'd experienced before. Each of us paused and inhaled the beautifully familiar sense that time itself was moving slower and that the King was among us in a special way. No doubt about it.

> We inhaled the beautifully familiar sense that time was moving slower and the King was among us.

Mollie bore the marks of someone in the midst of a battle. Chemotherapy had robbed her of her hair, and the tree of IVs next to her bed was feeding numerous tubes into her pale limbs. All the usual monitors and bits of technology were strung up behind her bed, but it was the other three walls that made me stop and stare.

They were covered with pieces of paper.

On each one was written a portion of Scripture. Some were printed; some were handwritten. Some were accompanied by drawings made with bright crayons; some had photos of people smiling back. Together they covered every possible bit of the three walls that could be seen from the bed.

Mollie told her story.

"My husband, Steve, and I have been through some tough trials over the years, and we always talked about how God allows them in our life to produce fruit or to take us to a new level of maturity. Over the last few years we've been asking the Lord, 'How are You going to use us? We want to be used in a powerful way for Your glory.'

"About a year ago, the Holy Spirit had laid on our hearts that something was coming. It was ominous, but not depressing. So we prayed and carried on doing what we do: being in the Word every day and taking any opportunity we could to talk to people about Jesus.

"I started feeling ill in the summer. I was exhausted and kept having these random fevers. I didn't know what it was but just assumed it was a typical season for a working mom with two kids. But even though we'd been talking a lot about having our faith tested, I didn't think my symptoms were in any way related.

"For years I'd been putting off a simple procedure on my eye, but earlier in the year I finally booked it in. Since they needed to put me under, I had some blood tests, which revealed that all of my blood counts were critically low. My eye doctor canceled the surgery, told me they'd never seen counts so low before, and told me to go to the ER. So after much discussion and prayer, Steve and I decided that I should visit the ER the following day to figure out what was going on.

"I went to the hospital the next day, and within a few hours I was told that they wanted to admit me as they thought I either had leukemia or another type of cancer. My world crashed down. Being told I had a terminal illness was terrifying. We were freaking out, and yet God's presence was there.

"Within a few days of diagnosis we knew this was it; this was what we had sensed was coming and for what we'd been preparing. All those conversations and prayers in the lead-up gave us a firm foundation to stand upon. There was a Charles Spurgeon devotion that I read the day before I was diagnosed. The theme of the scripture was 'He shall not be afraid of evil tidings,' from Psalm 112:7 [KJV]. I didn't realize at that moment that God was saying, 'Put on your seat belt. Things are going to change.'"

COVERING THE WALLS

George, Jonas, and I stood in silence, drinking in every word. Mollie pointed to one of the pieces of paper on the wall. Written in large, defiant black letters were the words: "LEUKEMIA IS NOT MY GOD." Mollie continued her story:

> Written in large, defiant black letters were the words: "LEUKEMIA IS NOT MY GOD."

"We knew this was an opportunity to teach our family. We talked with our children about how this was an opportunity to develop their faith at a young age, and what a privilege and honor it is to be tested in that way. We know that God has amazing plans for their lives, so much so that He is allowing them to go through this to strengthen their faith early on. But the only way we are going to get through this is by giving Him the glory.

"We believe that God wants to accomplish many things through this trial—some of the fruit we may never see ourselves. We are not going to give ourselves glory, and we are not going to make this disease our god—even though it's easy to let the disease become all consuming when our lives are revolving around being sick.

"Just a few days before I was diagnosed, Steve was praying and firmly heard the Lord say, 'I am going to heal your wife.' At the time, we figured it was a healing of something minor going on with my health. We did not realize He was promising to heal me of this deadly disease. At this point, we had a choice of whether we would doubt or believe God's promise.

"The only way I knew I would get through it was to constantly meditate on the Word of God. So I covered my walls with these Bible verses. Some I chose, while friends and family gave others to me. On the days when I'm too sick to open my Bible, these are the things that keep me going. I just lie here, stare at the wall, and read the Word to myself. That's how He ministers His comfort, peace, and reassurance to me."

Even though the first round of chemo hadn't worked fully and Mollie's only hope was a bone-marrow transplant, somehow she was full of reasons to be thankful to God.

"It's amazing how God used my eye doctor to get me to the ER—just in time. And even when I only had a partial response to the first round of chemo, I was learning to trust God. We were very concerned, and it was a huge testing point. We believed God was going to heal me, so why wasn't I in remission?

"I had to transfer hospitals that day, when I thought that I was going to be heading home waiting for a transplant. But we learned that it was easy to put Him in a box and tell Him how He was going to work. It reminded us of God's promise to give Abraham a son, and how Abraham contrived his own plan.

"I soon found out that the new hospital I was in is one of the best cancer hospitals in the world, and my new doctor is considered the pioneer of bone-marrow transplants. Within a couple of days, I'd heard so many employees tell me how fortunate I was to be admitted after just one day. They said people come from all over the world for treatment and sit on a waiting list for weeks and months. Immediately it was clear that God was reminding us to trust Him. He was in charge."

Mollie's second round of chemo put her in remission, but she had to stay in the hospital until her blood levels were safe enough. While she was waiting, she and her medics started talking about bone-marrow donors.

"Only a sibling can be a full match," Mollie told us, "and the chances of that happening are less than 25 percent. And I only have one sister. But my sister was a perfect match—ten for ten! The doctors were shocked and kept saying it was miraculous. But I knew that it was God saying, 'See, I am revealing My plan to you.'"

Eventually I brought out my guitar and started playing and praying. Jonas walked the room, reading out loud the verses on the walls. Mollie closed her eyes.

"Mollie," I said with a wink, "Jonas is a good worship leader. So is George. I do it for a living, so I guess I'm decent at it also." She smiled, not quite knowing where I was going with this. "But none of us are leading right now. You're the one leading all of us in worship in this moment. You're living through this crazy season, but you're so determined to bring glory to Jesus, to stand on the faith you have and sing Him a song in the night. That's what I call a worship leader."

So we sang. My fingers fumbled a couple of times, and our voices were a bit muffled under those yellow medical face masks. They cracked at times too, partly just being aware of the presence of Jesus in that hospital room, but also because we were so moved by Mollie's inspiring faith and example. We sang out with all we had, led by this amazing woman of faith.

> **You're living through this crazy season, but you're determined to bring glory to Jesus.**

Somewhere toward the end, Mollie looked up at the ceiling and exhaled. "This is an altar moment," she whispered. "Thank You, Lord."

Eventually it was time to go. As George, Jonas, and I said good-bye and walked out, I saw that beneath the words "LEUKEMIA IS NOT MY GOD," Mollie had written out a couple of verses from Isaiah:

> You will keep in perfect peace
>> all who trust in you,
>> all whose thoughts are fixed on you!
> Trust in the LORD always,
>> for the LORD GOD is the eternal Rock.
>
>> (26:3–4 NLT)

I carried those words with me as we stepped back into the corridor and took off our gowns, gloves, and masks. A nurse approached us.

"That lady in there is special, isn't she?"

The three of us just nodded and smiled back, unable to put into words quite how amazing Mollie was.

"Every day she's consistent," the nurse said. "Every day she's got that same joy, that same peace and determination to beat this."

AGAIN AND AGAIN AND AGAIN

I kept in touch with Mollie, and a couple of months later she gave me an update. The bone-marrow transplant had been grueling, just as she knew it would be. Even though every dividing cell in her body had been killed in preparation for the transplant, she was still trusting God.

When her plans to be home for Christmas fell through at the last minute, she was reminded of how God was in charge, and she once again chose to trust Him. A few days later, she was home and thankful for every single move of God's guiding hand in her recovery.

"I had a dream soon after your visit," she told me once. "I believe it was a spiritual one from the Lord. I was in the midst of a dark valley. It was cold, and as I looked behind me, I could see all these altars that had been erected. God was telling me, 'Look at how I've met you again and again and again since you've been in this trial.' I felt like He was telling me to keep walking one foot in front of the other. He was saying, 'You're almost at the base of the mountain.'

"The presence of God was so powerful when you visited. It was like having an out-of-body experience, and I felt like I had been taken to heaven for a little bit. After you left, I thought about how I never would have had that experience if I had not been sick.

"I think I finally understand what Paul meant when he said that he longed to go be home with the Lord, though he understood that he might need to be here on earth longer for other people. I've never longed for heaven so badly in my life. I'm kind of afraid of this trial ending. When it does, does it mean that His presence will diminish? I know as time goes by we could start getting lukewarm, and I grieve that thought. His presence is more desirable than anything."

In a moment like that hospital visit, it's always humbling to see the music accomplishing what I was hoping for when it was written and leading someone to connect with Christ in a special way.

There was a time when I used to feel a little frustrated with the songwriting process. Why was it that some songs I wrote would help people connect so well with God while others did not? And more to the point, why could I never really distinguish which was which during those moments of creating the song? You would think that after all these years I might be a little better at that aspect of things!

Besides, if you're spending your days leading people in worship, shouldn't you know about the basics of how it all works? Sure, I've learned a lot about the act of creating and crafting a worship song. You can learn to improve at getting out of dead ends, not over-repeating things, and staying within a melody range—all those kinds of things. But writing a song that connects with people on a deeper level in worship? Well, there's really no magic recipe for that. And at times in the past I'd found it hugely frustrating.

These days, however, I feel very differently. In fact, I celebrate the truth that there's no formula for writing a powerful worship song. I had no idea about "10,000 Reasons." I had about twenty songs for the album and just needed eleven. If it had been left solely up to me, I think I might not have even put it on the record—I wasn't completely sure if it was finished or not. In retrospect, considering all the beautiful stories that have come back through this song, I find it kind of hilarious. You'd think I'd be a bit wiser by now.

> If it had been left solely up to me, I think I might not have even put "10,000 Reasons" on the record.

Thankfully, my team intervened, with my producer Nathan memorably saying, "I don't care what song we're dropping from the album, but this one's going on!" That's what happened, of course, and by the time the record released, "10,000 Reasons" had become a central part of it, and the album title too. All to say, I was given a beautiful reminder of how little I actually know about all of this. And that doesn't worry me at all, because I've learned how my cluelessness can be turned into a brilliant way of the Father keeping me dependent on Him.

LIKE A HURRICANE

Oswald Chambers wrote that complete weakness and dependence are always the occasion for the Spirit of God to manifest His power. I love that. It's a swift reminder that even though God was kind enough to involve me and Jonas a bit in the process with this song, the stuff that really changes lives all comes from Him.

Learning what it means to be dependent while you're sitting in a chapel singing out your latest song ideas is like being in kindergarten. It's safe and it's basic. But it's a whole other level when you get to a place like where Mollie was—in that hospital room battling an illness she knew she could not defeat alone.

I was struck by the fact that she didn't seem desperate or depressed. She just seemed so dependent—totally, utterly, gloriously dependent on God. She surrounded herself with truth; she pushed back against fear by relying on God again and again. And she preached to herself with all the passion and persistence of a hurricane.

I walked out of her hospital room with more than a guitar that day. I left having learned from the example of an outstanding worship leader.

CHAPTER 6

THE ULTIMATE REALITY CHECK

Diane Lockhart told me how she had moved away from her home in Northern Ireland and spent two years living in Uganda. She partnered with a local gentleman, who had been brought up in the slums, to set up a project to help children in one of Kampala's poorest neighborhoods. Together they worked to grow the project into a school that was educating nearly two hundred children. These boys and girls woke up and went to sleep in dirty surroundings, with no clean water and a lack of safety. Diane, however, was inspired by how, despite these desultory surroundings, these children were still so intent on thanking God for all they had.

Then, shockingly, two years after returning to Ireland, Diane was diagnosed with breast cancer, and "10,000 Reasons" took on a special meaning for her. It became her theme song through all the hours of chemo, and as she tried to imagine the children waking up to a new day, it helped keep her focused on the goal of being back with them at some point.

I know it wasn't the song that was responsible for her worship—the song itself was just a vehicle for her to carry her trust and praise to the Savior. The source of her worship was a heart that had decided to keep Christ in the center, no matter what the circumstances.

Diane's now through the treatment she had back in her homeland, and she regularly visits the children in Kampala, where the song has taken on its own unique meaning. Since her return to Uganda, the children have learned to sing "10,000 Reasons." And whenever she hears them sing, the worship resounds more powerfully than ever.

> **The song was just a vehicle for her to carry her trust and praise to the Savior.**

STRAIGHT TO THE HALLELUJAH

A story like Diane's always interests me, for in the middle of her struggles with cancer, she didn't choose to sing a song about her health. She didn't choose a theme song that named her illness or focused in on the specific struggles associated with battling such a horrible disease. Instead, she picked "10,000 Reasons" as her theme, deciding instead to focus on the kindness and greatness of God and to bless His name. There's not a word in the song about cancer. It's all about Jesus.

One thing I learned quite early on as a worship leader was that, though sometimes it's useful to name the issues, it can be just as powerful when we don't. In other words, it can be powerful when we linger less on the "help me" stage of our songs and head straight to the "hallelujah" part. I'm not saying "help me" is an unimportant prayer—no, not at all. I'm arguing that "hallelujah" is often a very underrated piece of the equation. I believe there's a dynamic shift that happens inside of us, and in our situations, when we give more attention to the worth of God than we do to the worries of this world.

Worship is a window onto the heart of God. It's a way of seeing, not just a mode of singing. It's a place of illumination, not just a means of exaltation. Remember what Psalm 73 says: "When I tried to understand all this, it troubled me deeply till I entered the sanctuary … then I understood" (NIV). Things that made no sense to the psalmist suddenly came into focus when he fixed the eyes of his heart on God in a moment of worship.

Life can be so confusing and disorientating, especially when it involves suffering and struggle. At times we need some reassurance that there is a purpose and a plan and that someone at some point will make sense of it all for us. Worship can help complete the puzzle.

If you think about it, worship is the ultimate reality check. We're checking in with the reality of a

> **Worship is a way of seeing, not just a mode of singing.**

God who is on His throne and who will never be shaken. We're checking in with a King who reigns and rules forever and yet cares about the details of our everyday lives. We have all of our other realities going on—all the stresses and strains that can show up in this life, whether it is money issues, people problems, or whatever. But, as real and as relevant as those worries may be to us, in worship we check in with a reality that trumps them all. It is the reality of Jesus on His throne.

Worship must always take us to that place. As a worship leader I often remind people that we don't need to "get anything going" in that moment of leading worship, because we're simply joining in with something that is already happening. It is the eternal, heavenly song of Jesus, which now and forever swirls around His glorious throne. Scripture paints an amazing picture of that place; it describes angels in their millions, encircling and singing. There are elders bowing and living creatures speaking out praise upon praise. It's the grandest thing you could ever get involved with, and the most glorious song you'll ever get to be a part of. And there, right in the center of it all, is Jesus.

REARRANGING THE FURNITURE

Ron Owens explained that "when we come to worship, we come to a throne … [and] everything else arranges itself around that throne."[1] It's a perfect summary of how our lives work best too. For life to work as it was designed to, Jesus must be the focus, and we must shape our lives around Him. He must become the hub—central to all of our thinking, singing, speaking, and doing.

N. T. Wright took this theme further, saying, "Only humans it seems have the capacity to live as something other than what they are (God reflectors, image bearers). Trees behave as trees; rocks as rocks; the sea is and does what the sea is and does."[2]

In other words, though you and I were created to worship God, we have to choose to do it. Every other created thing will automatically perform whatever function it was created to do. But you and I, though we were made to be God reflectors and image bearers, have the capacity to wander away from that call and to arrange our lives around something or someone else instead. And as we do so, Jesus gets shifted off to the side, or maybe knocked out of the picture altogether.

In worship, we rearrange the furniture, making sure Christ is in the center place, where He belongs.

When we put something or someone else other than Jesus in that place of ultimate prominence, that thing becomes an idol. It is a fallen excuse for a god, with a string of false promises. C. S. Lewis said, "Idols break the hearts of their worshippers."[3] Whether it's sexual lust, the love of money, or an insatiable quest for a prestigious career and social status, if any of these things become our god, eventually they will consume us, fail us, or even break us.

We see it all the time—people sacrificing themselves on the altar of something that their whole lives now revolve around. It starts to consume them, and eventually relationships fall apart, family happiness fades, and even health begins to suffer.

> C. S. Lewis said, "Idols break the hearts of their worshippers."

Anything we bow down to will eventually gain mastery over us. It's not a matter of if; it's a question of when. Jesus, on the other hand, is a supremely kind master who always satisfies the hearts of His worshippers.

Wise hearts soon realize that not only is Jesus praiseworthy, but He is trustworthy too. There is no kinder or firmer a foundation to build our lives on. Life works best with Jesus on His throne in the center and everything else revolving around that throne. As He Himself taught us to pray, "Let it be on earth as it is in heaven" (see Matt. 6:10).

A DECISIVE CRY

Of course, it's easy enough to write these words down. It's another thing entirely to live them out. Sometimes life presents such turbulent circumstances that finding our way to the place of praise, and keeping Jesus central, is a huge undertaking.

It amazes me that in some of these life stories worship wasn't just something the person got around to later on, once they'd worked through some of the shock and pain. It was there in the mix, right there from the beginning. When the storm arrived, the instinct of their souls was not a defeated song of woe, but a decisive cry of worship. That's exactly what went through my mind when I received this email from Shirley.

> The instinct of their souls was not a defeated song of woe, but a decisive cry of worship.

Dear Matt,

Last night I received a text from a woman in my church. She saw that you are writing a book and encouraged me to submit and share my story. So as I sit and stare at the screen, I think ... how do I begin? I guess I just start on the day it happened.

October 29, 2013. It was mid-morning when my husband and I received word that Autumn, our three-year-old granddaughter, was being airlifted to a nearby city because she had fallen down the steps at the daycare provider's home. Upon arriving on the scene, the paramedics said she was unresponsive.

We dropped everything and drove the 70 miles. For the next two days we did not leave the hospital. The daycare provider came and was distraught, so we prayed with her there in the family room. The next day we found out that Autumn did not fall, but was the victim of child abuse and blunt force trauma at the hands of her daycare provider.

Autumn died late in the afternoon on the 31st. Our son and daughter-in-law entered a grief that was beyond words. We watched them and their two children, Faith and Jared, drive away from the hospital. Autumn's car seat was empty. Then we left too. Autumn's body remained. She was now a crime scene.

We were in shock, functioning in a daze. We had to wait to bury her, as an investigation was in action, but as we prepared to leave her celebration-of-life service and go to the cemetery, we stood in the church and sang the song "10,000 Reasons." The drummer belted out the drums and I felt my heart pound as the tears ran down my face.

The days passed and families went home, but the investigation was still under way. Every time we turned on the news we heard about our loved one. CNN. Nancy Grace. Dateline. They all approached us for comment. We heard it went international and saw articles in the London Times. *Whenever we were asked to speak about what had happened to Autumn, we wanted to be real and we wanted to show Christ. God gave us an opportunity to be witnesses to people in far-off countries in a way we never thought would happen.*

Thanksgiving came, and then Christmas, and those months were so hard. We had an empty chair. In the weeks ahead, as a mother I watched how all my children were doing. As a wife I was watching and caring for my husband. As a grandmother I was watching my grandchildren in their grief, and I was exhausted.

Six weeks after Autumn died, I used sign language in church to sign the song "10,000 Reasons." As I signed, I saw hands raised, tears flowing, and grief on the faces of the people in church. It was the end of December and I knew then that God was urging me to write throughout the year ahead.

So, starting January 2014, I wrote a daily Facebook message. I would ponder and share things that were hard and real, but I also shared blessings that God unfolded in each day. I decided to start every post with the words "10,000 Reasons ... Bless the Lord oh my soul ... " and then write about the day. I always ended, "Bless the Lord oh my soul ... "

At first I did not think I could fulfill my promise of doing it for a whole year, but in the end I found it to be an amazing journey. I prayed that it touched hearts and I just wanted to be obedient to Him.

Many times it was not easy, but I knew God wanted me to face my grief head on. I knew God wanted me to be real and honest. He wanted me to share about Him because so many other people face this kind of journey every day. Many become bitter and angry and they stay there.

I have found that this is part of my life now: seeing God's blessings even in the worst of days as well as in the best of days. He is there, giving treasures to us in many forms, and often we do not recognize them.

Autumn was a little girl who had a compassionate heart. She and her brother, Jared, were best friends. She was silly, loved camping, and savored marshmallows! She looked like a little chipmunk when she ate them. She loved her "Papa"—my husband—and would yell his name and run into his arms. She would sit by him and could charm him into almost anything. But most of all, she loved Jesus, and that gives us great comfort.

Autumn's story continues, both good and bad. The daycare provider is in prison, and a new local center is being put up for children to seek help from abuse, autism, grief, illness, and many other traumas that affect children. It's going to be called the Autumn Center.

God has used Autumn's short life on earth to touch many lives, and He continues to use her story to reach many people. We pray that many will come to know Him.

So, Matt, this is my story. A song played at my granddaughter's celebration of life, signed in church and used by God to fill me with phrases in a daily journal for an entire year.

By Grace Alone,
Shirley

Fanny Crosby's pen hadn't run dry even after writing seven thousand songs of worship.

The email was powerful enough in and of itself. I was so moved by how this dear family had walked through their dark valley with such a sense of dignity and faith. But when I came across Shirley's daily blog, I realized she wasn't done yet—she still had a song to sing.

It reminded me of the fact that Charles Wesley still had something to say as he uttered that final hymn on his deathbed. Fanny Crosby's pen hadn't run dry even after writing seven thousand songs of worship. And the psalmist himself declared, "I cannot stay silent." Shirley's blog reminded me of that exact same spirit.

It was day 365 of her entries, and her heart for Jesus was still beating strongly. Her soul, in the midst of all that suffering, was a deep well of worship.

> *December 31, 2014: 10,000 Reasons … the end draws near. In 15 minutes my year and 365 days of this will be done. Last year at this time I was nudged and convicted that God wanted me to do this. I started and really did not know if I would be up to this, but once I began I felt and knew that God had a purpose. My desire was to be obedient. Several times I felt like stopping, and then I would get that convicting nudge again. So what was His purpose? One thing in this year became very, very clear: I am nothing and can do nothing without Him. He is the air I breathe. He did not promise me that if I did this I would be free of pain. Quite the opposite. I have felt some persecution, but I have also known blessing.*
>
> *This was not really about me. It was about God. It was about a journey of one person walking with God. He allowed others to see the ups and downs of the journey.*
>
> *Is the journey over? Nope. But I can say this: it is a journey of hope. God will come back again and*

I will be with Him and will see and be with my granddaughter.

My heart's desire ... is that there will be those who will come to know the Lord through this. And with that I say, Bless the Lord oh my soul.

CHAPTER 7

10,000 YEARS AND THEN FOREVERMORE

He wasn't just a successful lawyer; he was also a senior partner in a thriving Chicago law firm with offices right by city hall. He was married too, with four daughters, a home in a prosperous part of town, and a thriving property portfolio. More than anything, he was a man defined by his faith. So when the great fire of 1871 tore through the city and turned his investments to ash, Horatio Spafford didn't despair or blame God. He added a "hallelujah" to his pleas for help. In the months that followed, he and his wife, Anna, devoted themselves to reaching out to as many as they could of the 100,000 people left homeless by the Great Chicago Fire.

For two years they worked to support others. Eventually they decided to take a break and made plans to travel to England with

Horatio's family and to accompany their good friend, evangelist Dwight L. Moody, on a ministry trip.

Just before they set sail, something came up at work. Not wanting to ruin the family holiday, Spafford persuaded his wife and daughters to go on as planned, saying that he would follow on later.

Nine days after he said good-bye, Spafford received a telegram from Anna in Wales. It began with the words: "Saved alone."

> **Spafford received a telegram from Anna. It began with the words: "Saved alone."**

The boat that his family had been traveling on had collided with another vessel. It sank, taking hundreds of people down with it, leaving only twenty-seven survivors. Anna fought desperately to save the lives of her precious daughters, yet all four died. Her last memory of the disaster was of her baby being torn violently from her arms by the force of the ocean waters.

Upon hearing the news, Horatio boarded the next ship out of New York to join his wife, taking the same route across the Atlantic. Toward the end of the journey, as the ship passed over the approximate area where his daughters drowned, he wrote the following words:

> *When peace, like a river, attendeth my way,*
> *When sorrows like sea billows roll;*
> *Whatever my lot, Thou hast taught me to say,*
> *It is well, it is well, with my soul.*

The song he penned that day, "It Is Well with My Soul," has gone on to become one of the best-known hymns the church has ever sung. It's not hard to imagine why: here's a man who journeyed through one of the most devastating life circumstances anyone could bear, and yet he walked through that valley with a song of trust and praise. The integrity and deep faith in his lyrics have resounded in the hearts of countless broken worshippers down through the decades.

Verse after verse, the hymn teems with the truth that helped Horatio stand in that moment. As the lines unfold, we hear him essentially saying, "I don't understand this, and the pain and sorrow are immense in this moment. But still, I will believe in a God of love; I will believe in His proof of that love on the cross. And because I believe that ultimately I am being cared for, I can say, 'It is well with my soul.'"

In the last verse he looks to the future. He knows that one day Jesus will return and that there will be an eternity with Him. He knows one day the clouds of suffering and confusion will clear, and Christ will make sense of it all:

> *And Lord, haste the day when my faith shall be sight,*
> *The clouds be rolled back as a scroll;*
> *The trump shall resound, and the Lord shall descend,*
> *Even so, it is well with my soul.*

Whenever I'm in a room of people singing this beautiful hymn, I can feel the unshakable hope of these words resounding in the hearts and souls of everyone gathered. It's interesting to note that the original lyric for that last line of the song was once "A song in the night, oh my soul"! Just like Paul and Silas and Andrew and Myu, Horatio Spafford was a worshipper who knew how to find his way to the place of praise even in the dark.

FRUITFUL IN THE LAND OF SUFFERING

For most of us, our own stories may not seem quite as dramatic or intense as those belonging to a man like Horatio Spafford. But we all have scars. I used to think of a scar as an ugly thing, something to cover up and be a little embarrassed of. The more I think about it, however, our scars are often the very things that make the story of Christ's work in our lives so real and relatable. They're also a deep reminder to us, the storytellers, of just how far we've come and the obstacles of pain, stress, or failure that we have overcome in Jesus. Scars are not just a record of our wounds. They are a display of our healing.

> Our scars are often the very things that make the story of Christ's work in our lives so relatable.

Our scars are signs of God's grace in our lives—signs that we've been through something and that we have made it to the other side. They remind us that we are not where we once were and that God has brought about a victory in our lives. Our wounds may have been deep and the night may have been dark, but the promise of God's love has been tested and proved in our lives. When we look back, yes we see pain, but more than anything we see provision and protection, and even the ways God has made us *fruitful in the land of our suffering.*

That phrase is straight out of the story of Joseph. It's a dramatic narrative, with many deep valleys and many high mountain places. It would have been easy for Joseph to feel bitter about all he'd endured—the beating by his brothers, the false accusations, and the unjust imprisonment. But seeing the fullness of all God had purposed for his life, and the position of favor he'd been entrusted with, Joseph looked back and saw nothing but grace. He named his second son Ephraim because it means "God has made me fruitful in the land of my suffering" (Gen. 41:52 NIV).

Thousands of years later, so many of us can see that same dynamic at work in our own lives. We see the kind wisdom and miraculous provision of God in our stories, somehow bringing good from the soil of our suffering. As C. S. Lewis observed, seeds often grow in dark places.

Not every trial or tragedy has a silver lining, and I know that even in my own journey there are things I don't think I'll ever really be able to make sense of this side of heaven. Yet perhaps we don't have to. To borrow from another Joseph phrase: in some moments we are fully aware that what the enemy meant for harm, God has meant for good.

But in the moments when we cannot see evidence of His hand, we have to trust His heart and know that He has not left us, that He is closer and more involved than we can begin to know. We have to learn to sing along with Spafford and his remarkable hymn—*it is well with my soul.*

Roger Dennison was a worshipper who knew how to do just that. After a three-year battle with stage IV colon cancer, he died and left behind three sons, ages thirteen, eleven, and nine. For some, it must have been so difficult to attend the funeral and come face to face with such pain and grief. But Roger had lived a life of thanks and trust toward God; he had died ready to leave all the suffering behind and spend eternity praising God.

When we cannot see evidence of His hand, we have to trust His heart.

Because of Roger's example, his oldest son was able to stand in that service and sing "10,000 Reasons" in front of everyone gathered. What a tribute, and what a testimony.

"It was beautiful," said his mother. She added that Roger's only regret was that he had not seen his boys grow into men. If they continue to follow Jesus with anything like that same attitude their father demonstrated, I'm pretty sure Roger's boys are going to grow up to be three truly wonderful men.

"I AM NOT AFRAID"

It sounds like Adam's father, Terry Ruehmer, was another worshipper who'd discovered the secret of saying "It is well" even in the midst of a storm. I heard from Adam on email, a while after his dad's funeral. I liked him from the outset as he told me that he thought he was the last person who would normally write such an email. He'd spent the last few years touring the world with a well-known mainstream rock band and every day read emails from strangers wanting to tell the band how much they liked one or another of their songs. "Still," he went on, "I felt like I needed to write this."

He told me that his dad had lost his battle with cancer earlier in the year. When his casket was leaving the church, Adam heard "10,000 Reasons" for the first time. He said he didn't really listen to the lyrics but found out afterward from his mom that it was one of his father's favorite songs.

A few months later, his mom sent Adam a DVD of his dad, who was a professional musician and music teacher, singing "10,000 Reasons" in church.

"It was the last performance of his life," Adam wrote. "This time I listened to the lyrics, and I got chills."

He thought back to something his dad had said soon after he had been told he was going to die. "I am not afraid," he had said. "I'm a Christian."

"I watch that DVD of him singing that song all the time. I'm so glad I have it and I hope the song means as much to other people as it does to me."

Of course, it wasn't the song itself that impressed Adam. The song simply gave his dad a way to showcase that beautiful, unwavering heart of faith that he was carrying.

> "I am not afraid," he had said. "I'm a Christian."

FAITH, HOPE, AND TRUST

These are just a few of the stories of people at the end of their lives
that have been shared with me after the release of "10,000 Reasons."
I've been sent a lot of testimonies like this, and I love how they all
share the same tone of faith, hope, and trust. Take the story of Tony
Grahn's twin sister, Tonya, who was killed in a church bus crash.
The youth pastor, his wife, and their undelivered baby were also
killed, and twenty-seven kids were injured. Tonya's departure left her
husband to bring up their five children, one of whom has Down
syndrome. It's hard to imagine how you would get past a tragedy
like that.

Days after the crash, Tony's son sent him a link to "10,000
Reasons." Somehow it helped soothe his soul in some of the darker
hours. Along with the many other ways God spoke into that moment
with grace and provision, Tony found his way through the wreckage
of this devastating incident to a place of hope and praise.

From the stories of Roger, Tony, and Terry to the other powerful
testimonies throughout this book, it amazes me to see just how resil-
ient a heart of praise can be. I find it awe inspiring how their songs of
worship were not overcome in the face of grief, loss, cancer—or even
a firing range. I often ponder that if we ourselves hear these stories
and find them so moving, poignant, and powerful, can you imagine
what they must mean to the heart of God? Can you even begin to
conceive how He might respond as He sees His beloved children
choosing to fix their eyes on Him and live out a life of trust and
adoration during their most traumatic and testing moments?

All of these people have something in common: even though they were inside the storm, they would not allow the storm to get inside of them. Some of them have been healed or delivered from their tough circumstances and live still on this earth to sing their stories of how God brought them their breakthroughs. Others breathed their last breaths here and went to be with Jesus—where, of course, they will be part of the eternal song.

Eternity is an important theme to highlight in our worship. So much of modern-day life is focused on the here and now. Some people won't look ahead because of anxiety about the future, while others are too caught up in the instant gratification of the moment to think about tomorrow and beyond. But worship reminds us of the big picture. It brings us back to focus on the God of yesterday, today, and forever, the One who was and is and is to come. Not only is He faithful for today, but He has a glorious tomorrow for us—or, as Adoniram Judson put it, "The future is as bright as the promises of God."

I like worship songs that remind us of this, and I think they're so important:

> *When Christ shall come, with shout of acclamation,*
> *And take me home, what joy shall fill my heart …*

> *When I stand in glory, I shall see His face …*

> *And I will rise when He calls my name*
> *No more sorrow, no more pain …*

When we've been there 10,000 years,
Bright shining as the sun,
We've no less days to sing God's praise
Than when we'd first begun.

Of course, that last one, from probably the best-known hymn of all, is what we were giving a nod and wink to in the last line of our little song:

And on that day
When my strength is failing
The end draws near
And my time has come
Still my soul will
Sing Your praise unending
10,000 years
And then forevermore

When we sing songs that point us toward eternity, they remind us that there is a plan and that there is a bigger picture. There is a God who is ever present in our stories, and for all the brokenness and confusion that clouds our souls here and now, one day we will encounter the fullness of His unfathomably bright majesty and mercy.

GOING HOME

Joan's sister, Patricia, was fifty-seven when she was diagnosed with esophageal and liver cancer. There were no signs that she was even sick, and the shock that her family felt was intense. Patricia's decline was rapid, and within weeks of being diagnosed, she was in absolute agony, days blurring into one another in the hospital.

"Patricia, what's your favorite song?" asked Joan one day when the pain seemed to be a little less excruciating.

Patricia smiled. "10,000 Reasons," she said.

The next time Joan came to visit, Patricia's condition had deteriorated. The pain was even more intense, but as Joan pulled out her phone and flicked to the song that she'd stored on YouTube, something changed within Patricia. Where there was agony, now there was peace. She started to sing, off key but without a care in the world. For the duration of the song, she lay still, hands in the air and worshipping.

> Singing songs that point us toward eternity reminds us that there is a plan and a bigger picture.

A few days later, just five weeks after Patricia was diagnosed, Joan and the rest of the family were told that Patricia had only a matter of hours left to live. They rushed to the hospital, all thirty-one of them squeezing into the little room. The family gathered to say good-bye, to tell Patricia that she was loved more deeply than she could ever know, and to sing her favorite song.

Some voices were loud; some hushed. Some faces were streaked with tears; some mirrored that same peaceful expression that Patricia still wore. Still they sang, still they prayed, still they reminded Patricia how much they loved her.

Among all those voices in that little room, one of them sang differently. It struggled to be heard, struggled to hold the tune, struggled as it fought for air. But Patricia sang out her praise unending with all the confidence and courage of one who knew she was finally going home.

GRADUATION

Kendra and her husband, Todd, experienced the kind of heartache that no parent should ever have to bear. Their son, Channing, died when he developed aplastic anemia, a disease in which bone marrow stops producing the necessary platelets and cells to maintain a healthy immune system.

It started one February afternoon when their normally healthy Channing came home from high school looking yellow. Kendra immediately took action, but when two hospitals realized they could not treat Channing, he was transferred to a third. Despite being a highly skilled and reputable hospital in the region, they could do very little as Channing's health deteriorated rapidly.

And yet, from his room came the sound of "10,000 Reasons." Days, then weeks passed, and Channing grew weaker, but still the song played.

It was on the morning of March 26 that Channing's parents were told that, among other insurmountable complications, their son was officially brain dead. Together with their two younger sons, Clay and Curt, as well as Channing's grandparents, aunts, uncles, and other family members, they surrounded his bed. Two of his aunts dialed in on separate phones so that they could be there too.

The family sang and prayed. Before long, doctors, nurses, and hospital staff entered the room too. With their heads bowed in prayer, they joined in the singing.

After an hour and a half, a close relative asked that "10,000 Reasons" be played. With the phone resting on Channing's stomach, all the voices in the room sang in unison. And during the song, Jesus chose to graduate Channing to heaven.

THIS IS NOT THE END

When Bryce stood up to deliver the eulogy at his dad's funeral, he knew he wanted to tell everyone who had gathered just how much his dad had changed. It had taken only a few years, but in that short period Bryce had watched his father transform from a hotheaded, strongly opinionated person to a mild, loving, open-minded, embracing father.

> During the song, Jesus chose to graduate Channing to heaven.

Bryce remembered the day his dad called the family to a meeting. His mother was in tears and the atmosphere tense. When Bryce looked at his dad's face, he saw something he had never seen before: sorrow. He listened as his dad spoke of the full-body checkup and the advanced lung cancer that had been diagnosed. And then, for the first time in his life, Bryce saw him break down and sob.

Even though the medics had given Bryce's dad a handful of months to live, somehow he managed to hang on much longer. Gradually, it became clear why. Bryce saw him begin to reach out to God, quickly finding strength, comfort, peace, and assurance in Him. Bryce also saw him put right a decades-long broken relationship with Bryce's uncle. Seeing grace and forgiveness in action like that was one of the most significant moments of all.

Years after the day when Bryce's dad had revealed his diagnosis with such sorrow, Bryce noticed a different look on his dad's face: joy. He knew it was all thanks to his new relationship with God.

As the treatment now started to fail, it seemed that God was slowly calling him home. Three years after Bryce had heard his dad say he was dying, it finally happened. Bryce arrived at the ward to see his dad gasping for air, one eye opened and the other closed. The entire family broke down in tears, and Bryce prayed out loud that God would comfort his dad and be with him through his pain. Soon, an aunt pressed play on his favorite song, "10,000 Reasons."

Bryce watched as both of his dad's eyes opened, fighting to remain so as he looked up toward something. When the song ended, the gasping stopped and his eyes slowly closed. He was at peace.

"Dad," said Bryce as he finished his eulogy, "I am saddened by the fact that you're no longer physically present to guide me further in life, to physically have a conversation together. But I know God's sovereign plan is a lot higher than my desires. I am greatly assured and encouraged that this is not the end of the story, that one day when my time comes, I'll see you again in God's renewed kingdom, where every tear will be wiped away, where there is only joy, where sorrow and suffering cease to exist."

"LET ME BE SINGING"

Fiona was pregnant with her first child when her husband, Mark, was diagnosed with ALS (also known as Lou Gehrig's disease, or motor neurone disease in the UK). The prognosis? All the evidence suggested that he would not make it beyond five years.

At first the couple was floored by the news. Mark had been so physically fit, and excelled at any sport he tried, from golf to table tennis, and even semipro football (soccer). Some of his goals became the stuff of legend among teammates and supporters. And yet his football friends all knew he was different. Afterward the team would often go out to celebrate together. When the drinks arrived, the tray typically held fourteen pints of beer and one pint of black currant and soda. Not that Mark had a problem with them drinking; he just knew it wasn't for him. He was never one to compromise on anything.

Mark's determination and desire to do all things well defined him. He was a dedicated, hard worker who devoted hour after hour to mastering whatever skill fascinated him. From the Rubik's Cube to playing the guitar, he had taught himself how to do it all brilliantly.

It was a terrible blow to be told that he would gradually lose control of his muscles and that over the

> **Right from the time of the diagnosis, Mark and Fiona agreed they would not stop worshipping.**

years his body would completely shut down. For some, it simply would have been too much to cope with, but Mark and Fiona were determined to search for the positives, no matter how faint the glimmer. Together they decided to trust Jesus for whatever was to come.

Mark and Fiona were worshippers, and right from the time of Mark's diagnosis, they agreed that they would not stop worshipping.

Along with many others, they prayed for healing. God was not silent. When they stood in front of their church and shared the news of Mark's diagnosis, God reminded them of the story of Shadrach, Meshach, and Abednego. As they entered the fire, these three men of faith announced that they believed the Lord had the power to save them. They also decided that even if God did not deliver them, they would not worship any other god.

Mark and Fiona agreed to do likewise: they chose to believe that God had the power to heal Mark, but that even if He didn't, they would worship Him through to the end.

"I felt like Mary," said Fiona, "cherishing things in my heart with each moment, knowing what was to come was not going to be easy."

When they first heard "10,000 Reasons," they sang passionately about wanting to still be singing when the evening came—no matter what lay before them. They both knew that, for Mark, the evening was coming a whole lot quicker than they ever had imagined. And yet, nothing could change their minds; they were going to keep on praising, no matter what.

One day Fiona asked Mark what he would do if he could have just one day off from his illness, to leave the wheelchair and the constant pain that plagued him every minute of the day. She knew that he missed being able to play sports and that he was desperate to be able to do all those things with their son. But his reply didn't include any of those activities.

"What I would want to do more than anything is to get out my guitar and lead people into the throne room in worship," he said. Worship music had always played a huge part in Mark's life. It had driven him to teach himself how to play the guitar, locking himself away for hours until he had mastered it.

He was just as diligent when he led at church, taking ages to prepare for a Sunday morning, always seeking the Lord. Though Mark loved the verse about God being a very present help in times of trouble (Ps. 46:1), he suffered some weaker moments when he wondered if he had done something to bring the illness upon himself. Even so, he had a deep enough knowledge of God as the loving Father to stop him from going too far down that road.

Worship music was a help to Fiona too. After the birth of their second child, she was in church one day singing "10,000 Reasons" again. Somehow the line from the second verse stood out:

> *For all Your goodness*
> *I will keep on singing,*
> *10,000 reasons*
> *For my heart to find*

Suddenly, Fiona was overwhelmed by an awareness of how good God was, even in the midst of intense pain. She thought of all the ways He had shown His love to them, despite the fact that Mark had not been healed.

Fiona thought about the incredible generosity of friends who had given them enough money to buy a house that would accommodate Mark's wheelchair. But the thought went deeper than that: more than what God had done, she was grateful for who He was.

> More than what God had done, she was grateful for who He was.

When she got home, Fiona told Mark that she wanted to start a Facebook page for people to write their reasons for singing of God's goodness. She called it "10,000 Reasons for My Heart to Sing." At the top of the page she posted a photo of Mark, looking weak and ill but still smiling.

With a four-year-old son and a two-year-old daughter, life was busy, and since Mark never lost his focus on the One who makes all things new, life was also happy. Even though Mark's body was getting weaker still, and he struggled to speak and was unable to do anything for himself, he continued to demonstrate God's love for others. Every person he knew talked about his incredible ability to make people feel like they were the most important person in the room, just because of his permanent smile. Smiling was just about the only thing that he didn't lose the ability to do.

Mark knew the pressure Fiona was under with looking after him and their two small children. Often he chose to suffer in silence rather than asking her for something, like scratching an itch or moving his hand for him. One of the hardest parts was the fact that his debilitating illness meant that everything in the family had to center on him, which was the last thing he wanted.

One of the final things he communicated to Fiona before slipping into a coma was that he wanted to go and be with Jesus and he wanted his wife to have her life back. Hard as things were, the life that she wanted was right there with Mark, illness and all.

In those final days the last verse of "10,000 Reasons" came into focus. Both Fiona and Mark knew that the day was approaching when he would be gone from this life. His strength was failing, and the end was definitely drawing near. But still his soul was singing.

Days before Mark died, the family gathered around his bed at home and sang all his favorite worship songs and hymns. After much singing and crying, someone said that they knew an angel had come to take him home.

Later, finally alone with her husband, Fiona held him in her arms and released him to go with the angel to Jesus. She thought about him standing before the throne, dressed in glory not his own—no more pain, no more tears. It was so painful and yet so joyful. She knew that on the road marked with suffering she had found a treasure so precious that the anguish became just a little more bearable.

> Fiona wouldn't want to be the person she was before the Lord revealed more of Himself to her through all the suffering.

Almost a thousand people attended Mark's funeral, many of whom would never have gone to church before. And the air was filled with the sound of worship.

At times Fiona still feels a bit like Mary, treasuring things in her heart, knowing the way that pain and joy are so often closely linked. She knows it probably won't be possible for her to fully understand why it all happened, but she also knows that the way Mark lived—and died—has drawn many people to the heart of God. And that he would be smiling about that.

Strange though it might sound, Fiona says she wouldn't want to be the person she was before the Lord revealed more of Himself to her through all the suffering.

"Of course I would love to have been able to learn what I have learned and still have Mark here. But I wouldn't want to go back and not have lived this life that in the end the Lord has allowed me to live so far. No matter what happens, whatever may pass and whatever lies before me, to behold the King changed everything."

THE END DRAWS NEAR

I once heard a midwife say that she thought death was really very much like birth. No matter how we go, either putting up a fight or in gentle surrender, there is still a loving Parent on the other side. Our loving Parent is waiting to scoop us up into strong arms and guide us through the new life ahead. That's a powerful image.

And on that day, wouldn't it be something to go with the grace, the courage, the trust, and the thankfulness that Mark, Myu, Andrew, Charles Wesley, and so many others have shown? And how more meaningful still if the adoring tone of that moment was simply a reflection of what our stories had already looked like up until that point? That we had navigated the storms of this fragile life with unshakable hope, unwavering trust, and a heart of unstoppable thanks and praise.

When the end draws near, our final breaths here on earth will flow into the very first notes of our song in heaven. Right now we count our blessings and name them one by one. On that day we will be counting them 10,000 by 10,000.

"10,000 REASONS"

Bless the Lord O my soul
O my soul
Worship His holy name
Sing like never before
O my soul
I worship Your holy name

The sun comes up
It's a new day dawning
It's time to sing Your song again
Whatever may pass
And whatever lies before me
Let me be singing
When the evening comes

Bless the Lord O my soul
O my soul
Worship His holy name
Sing like never before
O my soul
I worship Your holy name

You're rich in love
And You're slow to anger
Your name is great
And Your heart is kind
For all Your goodness
I will keep on singing
10,000 reasons
For my heart to find

Bless the Lord O my soul
O my soul
Worship His holy name
Sing like never before
O my soul
I worship Your holy name

And on that day
When my strength is failing
The end draws near
And my time has come
Still my soul will
Sing Your praise unending
10,000 years
And then forevermore
Forevermore

Bless the Lord O my soul
O my soul
Worship His holy name
Sing like never before
O my soul
I worship Your holy name

Bless the Lord O my soul
O my soul
Worship His holy name
Sing like never before
O my soul
I worship Your holy name

Yes I will
Worship Your holy name
Lord, I'll worship Your holy name

A Q&A WITH
MATT REDMAN

ON THE PROCESS OF SONGWRITING

Craig Borlase: Did you always know that you'd end up as a songwriter?

Matt Redman: No. When I was growing up, I had no clue what I was going to do in life as a job. But I thought I'd probably end up working with words in some way or another. I loved words, even from a young age at school. I loved wordplay and was writing poetry long before I wrote songs.

Scripture talks a lot about the power of words, and not just how we ourselves shape and use them, but how God does too. Psalm 33 tells us, "By the *word* of the Lord the heavens were made." What an amazing thought—that God just speaks and stuff comes into being. I love the idea that the forming of words is a big part of His creating process.

The first creative act of a human in Scripture is when God invites Adam to name the animals—so again, it's wordplay. God invites us into His creative process. He could have much more easily named them Himself, but it's a relationship thing—He's involving us in this creative activity.

In that moment, Adam becomes a wordsmith and wraps his words around what he sees—all these different creatures. It strikes me that in many ways we're doing the very same thing when we write these worship songs: God reveals something of His mercy or His holiness and we try our best to name it, to put some words together to describe what it is we're seeing. We never have to invent anything new—we're just wrapping our words around the nature and character of God, and all of His glorious acts.

CB: So you're a lyricist first and a musician second?

MR: I love music, and I can write some melody. But I've realized more and more it's the lyrics that I'm stronger at, and they're the aspect of music that most fascinates me. I'll much more likely wake up in the morning with a lyric going around my head than a melody. And I'm so blessed that I get to work with a lot of cowriters for whom the opposite is true—they bring a lot of melodic ideas to the table.

It's essential that the music is good, as an act of art, and as a way of people connecting with the song—but I think in a worship song, ultimately the music must serve the lyric. It's the words that will leave a lasting effect on people's hearts, minds, and souls.

One time in fifty someone will say to me that he or she has been touched by the melody or the music, but time after time it's the lyrics that are depositing something valuable in someone's heart. If songs are full of the truth of God, as revealed in His Word, they have power to change lives. When people say that a lyric helped them say something to God that they didn't know how to say, to me that's the ultimate encouragement.

CB: Does that add pressure to what you do?

MR: There is definitely a sense of responsibility. It can't just be all spontaneous overflow and outpouring—saying whatever comes to you in an unconscious flow of creativity. Worship songwriters have to take seriously the fact that they are dealing with the truth of God, talking to people about who He is—so there's a challenge to convey Him as well as you can. I'm aware that someone could walk into a church service and sing a couple of the songs and you're actually giving that person a picture of who God is. That's quite a responsibility.

Here's an interesting analogy—experts say that in the last fifty years, vegetables sold in the UK have lost on average 24 percent of their magnesium, 27 percent of their iron, and 46 percent of their calcium. So you think you're eating good, healthy food, and of course in some ways you are—but it's perhaps not as nutritious as you'd like to think it is.

I'm passionate that we don't get to that same place with our worship songs where things are exciting musically, there are new melodies and sounds coming through, but when you look at the overall "diet" it's not as healthy as you might think.

Apparently there's a link between the quality of the vegetables that are being farmed now and the quality of the soil; there just aren't the same nutrients in the soil as there used to be. It's all about what you're rooted in, where you're growing from—and worship songs have to be rooted in the Word of God. Rich songs will flow from songwriters who are exposed to the richness of God's Word.

CB: Where do you start?

MR: Well, of course you could just take a portion of Scripture and write a tune to it, but that's not an approach that I personally work well with. The best model for me comes from Eugene Peterson when he talks about prayer in his book *Under the Unpredictable Plant*. He describes the life of Jonah and the intense prayer he prayed when he was in the belly of that huge fish. Peterson says the fascinating thing is that not a word or phrase in that whole prayer is unique. It comes from the Psalms, and not just one or two, but lots of them, all muddled up together.

Jonah was being directed by the truth and revelation of God. It's a passionate overflow of the heart, but God's Word infuses every part of it. That to me is the ultimate model for songwriting. We need to be so familiar with the truth of God that in our intense moments of life, be that joy or pain, our songs of passion are infused by the revelation of Jesus, as found in Scripture.

CB: Do you ever look back on your songs and think they're lacking in nutrition?

MR: All the time. There are always things you learn, things you would have done differently. But the interesting tension of writing a worship song is that even before you start out, you know you're not going to fully achieve what you're aiming for, or entirely reach where you want to go to. Because of the subject matter we're dealing with, every song will fall short. We can't possibly capture the glory of God, the radiance of who He is, the depths of His mercy, and the heights of His grandeur and holiness in our simple little songs. There's no way.

In 2 Chronicles 2, King Solomon is about to build a great temple for God. A few verses later he says, "But who is able to build a temple for Him, for even the highest heavens cannot contain Him?" That same tension exists when we're writing worship songs. You've seen something of the glory of God and you want to portray Him as glorious and great, but you know deep down you can't contain Him in a song, or do Him justice in some words or a melody. You pour your heart out, you contend for music and lyrics—and give your best. You paint as big and true a picture as you can, all the time knowing it's just a hint, just a faint glimpse of who He really is. That's a healthy tension to live in as a songwriter—and I like being there.

I wrote to a number of pastors, preachers, and theologians a few years ago and asked what was missing in our worship diet—what were some of the missing ingredients and themes in our sung worship that we needed to do a lot better on. The number one answer they came back with was the Trinitarian nature of God. It's essential to our faith that God is perceived as Father, Son, and Holy Spirit, but if you look at the songs the church has been singing most in recent years, that ingredient has largely been missing.

CB: Why?

MR: My friend Christopher Cocksworth, Bishop of Coventry, said that sometimes an area like Trinitarian theology makes us feel nervous as songwriters; we see it as comparable to something like higher mathematics, only to be tackled by theological experts. But he said we need to have a little more confidence in these kinds of areas. For one thing, from the moment you became a Christian you became a Trinitarian theologian—because the Holy Spirit illuminated you as to whom Christ is, and then, in Jesus, and with Jesus, and through Jesus, you went to the Father. You got caught up in this mystery from that very moment. What a beautiful thought.

Once you start submitting songs for congregational use, you have to take these things seriously. You have to think about how you can best portray God—both with reverence and relevance. These days so many people get into writing worship songs through the route of music. That's not a bad thing, but it's interesting to me that a lot of the old hymn writers got into songwriting through the route of being ordained and trained in theology. The great need of the hour for us is theological accuracy—and a richness and depth in our songs that paints the big picture of who God is and what He has done, with as much color and creativity as we can.

We have to pay particular attention to this area. I heard one preacher tell songwriters, "Don't just tell us things are amazing. Tell us amazing things." In other words, don't just randomly use a load of superlatives about God—use them, but give them a context. List some of the reasons why He is so utterly worth worshipping—for example, His attributes, His works, His names, and His heart.

CB: Hymn writers have had a major effect on you?

MR: As a songwriter I'd say that outside of Scripture, they've probably been my greatest teachers. You see a guy like Charles Wesley who wrote all those thousands of hymns—but then backed up what he sang by spending his life on Christ. Or a hymn writer like Fanny Crosby, who overcame the challenges of her blindness with a life of worship, hope, and joy. Added to that, I love how they wrote on so many themes.

I read about one time when Wesley was caught up in a minor earthquake and apparently wrote "no less than 17 hymns" in response—all speaking into the moment. He wrote of how the things of this earth are so fragile, temporary, and likely to fail us—but the things of God are eternal and unshakeable.

One more example—the poet and hymn writer Frances Havergal—most well known for her hymn "Take My Life and Let It Be." She lived through a lot of illness and physical pain, and died at the age of forty-two. But, strikingly, one of her main themes was the sovereignty of God. My favorite is a piece called "Disappointment." One of the song's twenty verses says:

> *Our plans may be disjoined*
> *But we may calmly rest;*
> *What God has once appointed*
> *Is better than our best*

Those four simple lines have such deep truth to them. The verse doesn't mention the sovereignty of God directly, but it unpacks that grand theme in an inspiring and poetic way. The best thing of all to me is there's nothing complicated about it—and yet it has an inherent depth to it. It's both deep and accessible. I think that's the challenge for every worship songwriter—to be able to write a song that's simple but by no means shallow.

Another great example is William Cowper, who wrote the hymn "God Moves in a Mysterious Way." It's one of the best hymns to tackle that theme of the sovereignty of God—the sense that Jesus rules and reigns over every detail of our lives and has a plan. I love lines like these in that old hymn:

> *His purposes will ripen fast*
> *Unfolding every hour*
> *The bud may have a bitter taste*
> *But sweet will be the flower*

What impresses upon me the most is that these words were written by a man who had huge struggles with depression. So not only are these words poetic and deep—they are also a sacrifice of praise. He's standing in the place of his affliction, and with the writing of this hymn saying, "I believe You, God—and I believe in Your sovereignty." So it's not just some clever writing—it's coming from his life. It's a gutsy, costly confession of trust and praise, against all the odds. Time after time many of these old hymns and their stories teach us so much about what it means not only to write songs of worship, but also how to live lives of worship.

CB: There's a well-known video of Eugene Peterson and Bono discussing the Psalms. Bono says that he is "suspicious of the lack of realism" in modern worship. Do you believe anyone who knows your story, or who has read this book, will know that your songs are always personal?

MR: The nature of how I got into this is that the songs were my way of processing some pain, so I've always had an element of realism in there. And I've always noticed that it connects most with people when I try to write songs that way. The trick is to be personal and passionate, so that the song is a raw overflow of the heart—but at the same time, don't be so specific that people can't attach their own stories to the lyric.

Worship should address the whole of life—the highs and the lows, the struggles and the joys. And you can find everything you need for that within the pages of Scripture.

I once heard a guy named Gerard Kelly say, "If you think that the idea of rooting songwriting in Scripture is restrictive, then you don't really understand what Scripture is." I think he has a point. It's easy to sanitize things, to dial down what we feel because it sounds too full on. But maybe we should have some more extremes. There's rage in the Psalms, but I've never heard rage in a modern-day worship song.

Now it's not a straightforward subject, because of course as well as wanting things to be real and raw, we're also trying to help everyone travel together and keep things as congregational as possible. But take the example of injustice—that's a subject we could all unite around, and we could all sing a worship song that spoke of God's (and our) anger against injustice. So many streams of the church these days have really stepped up their efforts to be a force for good, and stand up for the marginalized, the downtrodden, and the oppressed, reflecting God's heart for social justice.

So maybe some of these themes should show up in our songs too. How about we sing of how Jesus turned over the tables in the temple, raged against the unjust practices of the moneylenders there, and compared it to something that happens in our society today? The point is we need to depict as much as we can of the whole character of God, who is a roaring lion as well as a sacrificial lamb. It's back to what we spoke about earlier—painting the whole picture and not presenting people with a God who is passive or disengaged.

The tragedy would be if people heard all this passionate, raw music outside of church and then when they stepped into church they found that we just sounded bored about God and lethargic about life. Worship songwriters need to be both passionate and purposeful: passionate in that their songs explode with emotion and energy, but purposeful in that the songs are crafted in such a way to help people see a true picture of the matchless God of glory and grace we find revealed in Scripture.

CB: What would be some songwriting wisdom for young worship songwriters to think about?

MR: The number one thing is to let other people into the process. It can be very easy as a creative person to want to do it all yourself. Honestly, I used to have that approach. I was too sensitive about my songs and not vulnerable enough to allow other people to speak into the development of a song.

It can feel easier to work alone, as you don't have to let your guard down or negotiate. But it's so much better to actually invite people in to comment on stuff, to give truthful responses to what you're working on—and of course to cowrite and collaborate. It's far too big a challenge to attempt on our own. If we're going to dig deep theologically and creatively, we'll need to realize we are "better together."

We can sharpen one another to become better songwriters, and better worshippers. Almost every song I write these days is a cowrite, and I'm aware time after time that I would never get to where a song ends up without other people's input and perspective. The song "10,000 Reasons" is a huge example of that—the way it was birthed speaks so much about collaboration; it came from a friendship and songwriting partnership that we'd really invested in.

CB: What's the greatest challenge of being a worship songwriter?

MR: The main challenge is to make sure that what we're singing or writing about never becomes divorced from what we're living. Music is an amazing part of God's blessing and presence in this world, and it's a powerful way to speak to God in our worship—but it's never enough on its own. We can't attempt to write great new songs with great new sounds, but then have our lifestyles be inconsistent with what we're singing.

As Augustine warned, "Do not let your life give evidence against your tongue. Sing with your voices, sing also with your hearts. Sing with your mouths, sing also with your conduct."

Sometimes when you're singing a worship song it can feel like such a precious and valuable moment with God. But you have to remind yourself that it's only truly valuable if you go from that place and live out what you're singing. As I always remind myself, singing is relatively easy—the proof is always in the living.

NOTES

CHAPTER 1: 10,000 REASONS FOR MY HEART TO FIND ...

1. Mario Cacciottolo, "The Cornish Beaches Where Lego Keeps Washing Up," BBC.com, July 21, 2014, www.bbc.com/news/magazine-28367198.

CHAPTER 2: PREACH TO YOURSELF

1. Martyn Lloyd-Jones, *Spiritual Depression: Its Causes and Cure* (Grand Rapids, MI: Eerdmans, 1965), 20.

CHAPTER 6: THE ULTIMATE REALITY CHECK

1. Ron Owens, *Return to Worship: A God-Centered Approach* (Nashville: Broadman and Holman, 1999), 53.

2. N. T. Wright, *The Case for the Psalms: Why They Are Essential* (New York: HarperOne, 2013), 120.

3. C. S. Lewis, *The Weight of Glory* (New York: HarperOne, 2000), 31.

BIBLE CREDITS